Traditional Highland Dress

Traditional Highland Dress

A Comprehensive Illustrated Guide

Second Edition

by

E. L. Roberts-MacDonald
of Abrone, FSA Scot

With an introduction by

Pam Blackhall,
Kiltmaker

Palfrey Press

Copyright © 2024 by Ethan L. Roberts-MacDonald. All rights reserved.

Copyright is retained for all the illustrations and text in this publication by the author and the individual contributors. Use of the arms are further protected by the laws of their specific granting authority.

In accordance with the U.S. Copyright Act of 1976 the scanning, uploading, and electronic sharing of any part of this book without permission of the author constitutes unlawful piracy and the theft of the author's intellectual property. If you would like to use material from the book (other than for review purposes), prior written permission must be obtained by contacting the publisher art permissions@palfreypress.com. Thank you for your support of author's rights.

This publication is designed to provide accurate and authoritative information in regard to the subject matter covered. It is sold with the understanding that the author is not engaged in rendering fashion, lifestyle or other professional services. While the author has used his best efforts in preparing this book, he makes no representations or warranties with respect to the accuracy or completeness of the contents of this book and specifically disclaims any implied warranties of merchantability or fitness for a particular purpose. This book is designed to provide a broad overview and insight into the topic of traditional highland civilian dress through text, photographs, and illustrations. While the publisher and author have used their best efforts in preparing this book, they make no representations or warranties with respect to the accuracy or completeness of the contents of this book. Neither the publisher nor the author shall be liable for any loss of profit or any other commercial or personal damages, including but not limited to special, incidental, consequential, personal, or other damages. To the maximum extent permitted by law, the publisher and the author disclaim any and all liability in the event any information, commentary, analysis, opinions, advice and/or recommendations contained in this book prove to be inaccurate, incomplete or unreliable, or result in any investment or other losses. Your use of the information in this book is at your own risk.

Illustrations and Cover Art by Heikki J. Halkosaari

Second Edition: 2025
First Edition: 2020

Hardcover ISBN: 978-1-960736-01-7
eBook ISBN: 978-1-960736-02-4
Library of Congress Control Number: 2024944168

Printed in Columbus by Gatekeeper Press

Published by Palfrey Press (www.palfreypress.com) in Northport, Maine

I dedicate this book to my grandfather and all those who have supported the creation of this work.

Forward

Scottish highland dress, while instantly recognizable by its tartan patterns and kilt, is far more than just a fashion statement. It is an emblem of the strength and resilience of the Scottish people, a testament to our enduring spirit, and a celebration of our unique culture. From the simple, functional garments of early Gaelic society to the intricate, symbolic attire of today's formal wear, highland dress has evolved to reflect the changing times and tastes, while always retaining its roots in Scottish tradition.

In this meticulously researched volume, Ethan MacDonald delves into the origins, history, and significance of each element of highland dress, and provides practical guidance on what to wear when. Weaving together historical accounts and expert insights, Ethan sheds light on the craftsmanship, symbolism, and cultural importance of the iconic garments that make up traditional highland dress. He has been thoughtful to also include women's fashion in this guide as well, an important topic so often overlooked in many other works on this subject.

Whether you are a seasoned sartorialist, a newcomer to the world of highland dress, or simply someone who appreciates the beauty and complexity of traditional clothing, this book is sure to inspire you. As you immerse yourself in the rich tapestry of Scotland's worn heritage, may you come to appreciate the enduring legacy of highland dress, not only as a stunning and distinctive form of attire, but also as an expression of the indomitable Scottish spirit. I invite you to embark on this journey through the world of traditional Scottish highland dress.

Pam Blackhall, Kiltmaker
Tarland, Scotland

Preface

This Second Edition of *Traditional Highland Dress* is in actuality a heavily revised and updated version of my earlier publication *Scottish National Dress: a Traditional Highland Perspective*, which was published in the summer of 2020. Much of it has remained the same, however, several chapters have been removed or merged with existing chapters and new chapters on different topics have also been added, along with updated artwork, photos, and appendices. It is my hope that this new publication will better serve as a guide for those interested in the subject of Traditional Highland Dress. This book is being released after the bicentennial anniversary of King George IV's state visit to Scotland, an event which is often seen as the beginning of the Highland Revival, and where, over the course of about a hundred years, the conventions of the 18th and 19th centuries combined to create the modern Scottish National Dress that we see today in the 20th and 21st centuries.

E.L. Roberts-MacDonald, 2024

Table of Contents

Forward vii
Preface ix
Appendices xiii
Acknowledgments xv

1. Defining Traditional Highland Dress as Accepted Today ... 1
2. Tartan and Tweed 5
3. The Kilt, Tartan Skirts, and Trews 13
4. Sporrans and Other Accessories 21
5. Determining What to Wear based on the Occasion 39
6. Casual Wear 43
7. Daywear 49
8. Highland Dress for the Sportsman and Hiker 61
9. Morning Dress or "Smart Daywear" 69
10. Eveningwear, Black Tie and White Tie 75
11. Headgear 95
12. The Plaid 105
13. Closing Words 113

Appendices 115
Glossary of Terms Associated with Highland Dress 139
Sources 147

Appendices

Appendix A: A Reference Guide for Dress

Appendix B: The Scottish Clans and their Chiefs

Appendix C: Scottish Armigerous Families

Appendix D: Plant Badges

Appendix E: A Guide to Ladies Tartan Sashes

Appendix F: The Wearing of Decorations and Awards with Highland Dress

Appendix G: Highland Wear "Under Arms"

Glossary of Terms Associated with Highland Dress

Sources

Acknowledgments

Creating this work would not have been possible without the tireless work of a great many individuals who helped in research, proofreading, donations, photo contributions, and artwork. All of you have my eternal gratitude. I'd especially like to thank Ian Boden for starting me in my Highland Dress journey. Tom & James Mungall, Harold Canon, Nathan B. MacDonald (FSA Scot), Glen Allardyce, Jeffery Foster, Caleb Burch, Isaac Walters, Paul Henry, Kyle MacPherson, Stanley Bird, Kevin Conquest (MStJ), Dr. Zaw-Htet (MRCGP), and Eric McCracken for their extensive subject knowledge, research help, general advice, and photo contributions over the years. Beth Tharpe Baucom, Devae Tharpe, Aurora Burton, Shelby Burton, and Anna Allman for their photo contributions and their assistance with ladies fashion and photographs. Alexander Cave for the use of his photos and advice on jackets. I would also like to thank James MacPherson of Cluny, Brady Brim-DeForest of Balvaird Castle (FSA Scot), and John Wright of Deerfield for the usage of their crest badges in illustrations. Brady Brim-DeForest of Balvaird Castle, Alex Gury, the Wright Family, the Tharpe Family, and several other individual donors who assisted in fundraising for the publication. As well as Kenneth Mansfield, Carrolin Bliss Wiggers, and Gage Garlinghouse who were kind enough to be my initial editors, proofreaders, and assistant wordsmiths. And finally to my publisher, Palfrey Press, who has worked tirelessly through our sundry revisions and renditions to make this dream a reality.

Introduction

Traditional Highland Dress has always fascinated me. Growing up, my Scottish roots were always highlighted by my family, and between them and a large local Scottish community, my love for the subject was kindled. My passion for it was cemented at age 15 when I purchased my first kilt to wear at our local scout camp for "Kilt Fridays", organized by a friend and mentor. Shortly after this, I began engaging in various online groups and reading much from historical and contemporary sources. Eventually, with the help of friends, I established my own online community, dedicated to the study and sharing of Traditional Highland Civilian Dress (THCD). This book was written as a guide for those who are on the beginning of their journey with THCD, and as a useful reference for those who have been dressing in traditional highland civilian style for decades. Here I will do my best to explain the common conventions, origins, and traditions of Highland dress. It is important to know that THCD is not a costume to be worn by reenactors, nor a uniform; but a form of National Dress which has evolved over many centuries of wear, only coming to its present form after many centuries of refinement. By wearing and studying it we keep our Highland Traditions alive for generations to come.

Defining Traditional Highland Dress as Accepted Today

Defining what is and what is not Traditional Highland Dress, especially in regard to civilian dress, can be a very complicated endeavor. If you ask five different people, you may get five different answers, so it is important to keep an open mind, as traditions do evolve. With men's fashion especially, that evolution can be quite slow. That reality, when coupled with the idea of Highland Dress as a national or ethnic dress, adds to the subtlety of the changes in Highland wear over time. If you look at Highland Dress in the past hundred or so years, you will see that it has not changed drastically. But, the Highland garb of the 18th and early 19th centuries varies wildly from that of today as our idea of Highland wear is the product of the interwar period – where modern men's fashion, with elements of the late Victorian and Edwardian styles, fused.

Since the 1920s, Highland fashion has solidified into what we know today as Traditional Highland Civilian Dress (THCD). This gradual change in style can be seen through photographs of both the gentry and everyday Scots. So, it would be fair to label 1919–present as the scope of what we call Traditional Highland Dress. Since the late 1990s and early 2000s, there have been many modernist trends that have been seen by some as a part of standard Highland dress, but those trends should be more properly labeled as contemporary style or, possibly, simply fads. These newer fashions, which have been pushed by several retailers, have led to confusion about what is "proper" in regards to Highland wear and have also led to the idea that traditional Highland wear is "vintage" wear. This is simply not the case, as the traditional style is still the prevalent form of Highland wear in Scotland and in the greater Scottish diaspora.

THCD does exclude some items that, in recent years, have seen increasing popularity. Items such as great kilts (which are almost always modern tartans and in extremely light weight fabrics), the "Jacobite" shirt, and the so-called "Lairds vest" can only be described as farbish, as there is little historical precedent for them in our era. These items have only arisen due to the romanticized and historically incorrect Hollywood portrayal of Scottish Highland Dress and fall heavily short of true Highland wear.

Victorian and Edwardian fashions are similarly inappropriate in THDC. While the fashions of those periods did heavily influence the Highland Dress of today, many items would be blatantly out of place. That is not to say that certain items and accessories of the period should not be worn with current THCD – quite the contrary! If one has a sporran, belt, sgian dubh, or dirk of the period, I encourage and expect you to wear it. The use of these heirloom quality items keeps the tradition alive and are a great addition to any outfit, albeit in a limited way. Later chapters will more accurately define what items fit into THCD based on the formality of an event and the time of day. They will also include many photographic examples to serve as a helpful guide.

Tartan and Tweed

Tartan

Tartan and tweed are the bedrock of all Highland Dress. Tartan, which has gone through many years of evolution to get to its present state, has a very interesting history. But before getting into the story of tartan, we must take a brief look at the peoples who are most commonly associated with it: The Celts.

Tartan, or more specifically plaid, has existed for thousands of years, and was common throughout the ancient world, especially in the lands inhabited by the Celts and other Indo-European cultures. It should be noted that modern usage of the term "Celt" to identify modern Scots and Irish people is a great misconception. The terms "Celt" and "Celtic" both being widely misattributed to modern and historic people groups. This is mainly a product of the 19th century, and to some extent early nationalist movements in areas that at one point were home to Celtic cultures. The terms are mainly used today, in academic settings, to refer to cultures that had common artistic styles, languages, and other similarities; and not, on the whole, to refer to a specific ethnic group. It is true that over time, many of these groups homogenized and condensed to specific geographic areas; however, as they did this, the specific identity became an Ethno-Linguistic one. Referring to modern Scottish, Irish, and Welsh peoples as "Celtic", either by culture or ethnicity, doesn't make much sense in a historical context; as these historic populations ceased to be wholly Celtic in their material culture around the 4th and 5th centuries, with the influx of Anglo Saxon and other Germanic peoples over the next several centuries. Evolving into the precursor cultures of the modern Scottish, Irish, and Welsh peoples . The greatests holdovers from this old Celtic world are still seen to this day in their modern successor cultures, these things being the Celtic languages…and tartan.

I am not saying that the Celts had anything akin to our modern understanding of tartan, only that tartan-style fabric has been common in this region for a long time, and the basic idea of it is ingrained into the culture.

The first kilts and trews that were common in the 17th and 18th centuries were "tartan", but not tartan as we think of it today. One can describe this idea of early tartan similar to how we have local or "district" tartans today. A local weaver would have made their own pattern which would have been worn by many in the area, without it being considered a mark of allegiance to any Clan or family.

Another aspect of the history of tartan that we should consider is the idea of the "Tartan Ban" in the aftermath of the failed Jacobite Rising of 1745-46. In instances like this, it is important to differentiate history from cultural memory. The latter being in most people's minds; that after the war, the English oppressors outlawed all tartan, confiscating and burning kilts as they went. This was done as a part of The Disarming Act of 1746 (also known as the Acts of Proscription). There are many controversies around this act and indeed around this time of Highland history, so I feel it is important to look at it directly. The following section of the "Disarming Act of 1746" said that it was illegal for men and boys to:

"Wear or put on the Clothes, commonly called Highland Clothes; (that is to say, The Plaid, Philebeg or Little Kilt, Trows, Shoulder Belts, or any other part whatsoever of what peculiarly belongs to the Highland Garb, and that no tartan, or party-coloured Plaid or stuff, should be, used for Great Coats or for Upper coats"

As you can see, this act still allowed for women to wear Highland garb as done at the time (women in the highlands were mainly wearing the standard fashion of Western Europe at the time but often wore the Airisaid — a tartan shawl that was sometimes worn as a dress or outer skirts), and exceptions were also made for the gentry and the army, allowing men of this class to wear the kilt. As the act more so had to do with the disarming of the everyday man and removing the clan identity (as the clan system functioned mainly as a militia, and these units made up a large part of the Jacobite army). So the wealthy elite were mainly exempt, as were the professional Highland regiments, who continued to wear kilts; both of these groups to a large extent were also Hanoverian aligned. While men were generally not allowed to wear kilts and tartan, its use didn't die out quite as we think it did. There is also much evidence that a few years after the act's passage, the enforcement of it wasn't as heavy handed as it had been in the immediate aftermath of the rising.

The act also was only to be enforced in the Highlands; the Lowlands were excluded. So tartan in Scotland, while suppressed, was still a large part of the material culture. I feel that this myth has often been heavily reinforced as fact due to the many romantic works of authors like Sir Walter Scott and others who, for the most part, molded the Highland Revival of the early 19th century. These works, as well as the many modern ones, such as the movie "Braveheart" and the book series and television show "Outlander" have led to many misconceptions about the various movements and fashions throughout Scottish History. While these works are good and enjoyable, it is always important to remember that they are entertainment and not history.

This was thankfully not the end of tartan, as in the beginning of the 19th century, a romantic revolution was sweeping the world. As said above, history and myth became one for the purposes of books, art, and of course, fashion. The Highland Revival of the early 19th century was the beginning of what we see as Highland culture today.

The Disarming Act was repealed in 1782, but Scottish culture had been decimated, and this revival 20 years later brought new life into the land. The works of authors like the aforementioned Sir Walter Scott, brought an air of mystery and chivalry to every aspect of Scottish culture, including tartan. The idea of tartan as a mark of one's clan or family started here as well. Well regarded weavers such as Wilsons of Bannockburn, who to this day are known for producing some of the most beautiful tartans ever woven, or more questionable characters such as John Carter Allen and Charles Manning Allen – the infamous Sobieski Stuart brothers – with their books, "Vestarium Scotium" and "Costume of the Clans", which were, for the most part, blatant nonsense, and impacted designs that still exist to this today. Either way, tartan and Highland Dress came back in fashion, and this was made even more apparent with the 1822 state visit to Scotland by His Majesty, King George IV, where the King was clad head to toe in Highland garb, surrounded by clan chiefs and the tartan-clad Royal Company of Archers.

As many well know, once the royal family picks up a new trend, everyone else does as well; so throughout Scotland, tartan was being produced en masse. George IV was not the last monarch to follow the trend; later Queen Victoria and her consort, Prince Albert, fell in love with all things Highland.

Prince Albert himself is credited for designing and registering many tartans for his and his family's usage; as well as the devising of estate tweeds to be worn at Balmoral Castle, the

Royal Family's private Scottish residence. Queen Victoria was an avid admirer of all things Scottish. She painted scenes and landscapes, learned Scots Gaelic, and even described herself as a Jacobite.

The Victorian Highland Revival is still present in almost every aspect of Traditional Highland Dress today. As far as tartans, there are many designs to choose from; you can even design your own. The most common way to wear a tartan though is to wear that of your own clan – this is seen as the most traditional and logical choice. Your clan tartan is, in the end, whatever your chief says it is. There are of course several non-clan tartans to choose from as well, many specifically made for organizations or local districts, and some even national tartans. You may also wear the tartan of another clan simply based on its beauty. I would suggest however that if you are attending a gathering or function for your clan, you do not wear the tartan of another clan. If you wish to research tartans based on clan affiliation or area, the Scottish Tartans Authority is a good place to start. Otherwise your clan or society website should have information on your clan's tartan or more specific variants.

Tweed

There is another fabric that is just as common and just as important as tartan: Tweed. Tweed, like tartan, is a wool fabric that is woven in a special way. There are many patterns as well, with the most recognizable being Herringbone and various

Checks (including houndstooth and barleycorn). While in recent fashion, simpler and more muted tweeds are the norm, tweeds have often been quite loud or busy in their own right. And just as tartans have been woven for different groups, so have tweeds. These are often for various Highland regiments, estates, and community organizations and associations.

Tweeds are mostly used for the making of jackets, waistcoats, and trousers, but have also been used for making kilts (even tweed can be coloured as tartan). The tweed kilt has recently become popular again with newer fashions; though it should not be discounted as a new trend. As there are many examples of tweed kilts going back to the late Victorian and early Edwardian eras. Whatever the fashion may be, I expect that tartan and tweed are here to stay as the bedrock of Highland Dress.

III

The Kilt, Tartan Skirts, and Trews

The Kilt

The kilt is arguably the most important part of all Highland dress. Its basic form, as far as we practitioners of Traditional Highland Dress are concerned, is fairly standard. It takes its shape as a pleated skirt, worn at the true waist or slightly higher, its hem rests just above or at the knee, and it can be made of a variety of woolen materials, but is most commonly made from some form of tartan or tweed. The kilt can be fastened in many ways, but is most commonly done via a set of two or three straps and buckles or by woven ties (though these are quite rare today), and may be pleated in many ways. The yardage is also variable, with anywhere from four to eight yards of fabric being standard. The yardage does not make a kilt a "true kilt," as some have said in the past, mainly as peoples waist sizes are different and for a kilt to fit properly it may need to be below or above the normal yardage based on a person's size. This coupled with the fact that many kilts of the Victorian and Edwardian era were normally low-yardage kilts, using only about four to five yards total – a phenomenon that continues as standard practice to this day, however, the amount of fabric does play a role in determining the style and depth of pleating for the back of the kilt; with knife and box pleats being the most common. No style is more traditional than another, though historically, box pleats were more popular in Victorian circles, while knife pleats gained popularity in the Edwardian era and are still seen as the primary form of pleating on kilts today.

Both five- and eight-yard kilts have their advantages. Obviously eight yards being more fabric weighs more; giving it a heavier and bolder cut, as well as a nice sway as you walk. Five-yard kilts are better suited in warmer climates, as they are lighter, and they also are the more affordable option for many. I personally find five yards more comfortable for extended use and wear, but this is of course my personal opinion.

The next image shows the three most common forms of pleating: Knife, Box, and Double Knife. These three pleating styles can also be used for ladies tartan skirts of any length. The following image shows the tartan pleated to the sett, but in both a five- and eight-yard arrangement.

*The three most common forms of pleating:
Knife, Box, and Double Knife*

Tartan has several parts with their own names, like a cell, multiple parts come together to create the larger piece. The two main terms one hears however are Sett, and Stripe. The stripe is very obvious, it is the predominant vertical line in the pattern. When pleated if one sees the lines across the back like columns then it is pleated to the stripe. The sett however is a section of the pattern, normally it is symmetrical and repeats over and over; there do exist some asymmetric tartans however, these include.

*MacPherson Tartan Pleated (from the top down):
to the Sett, Double Yellow Lines, Grey Block, and Black Block*

Tartan Skirts

Tartan skirts for women are far less regimented. They can be cut like a kilt – that is to say, knife or box pleated in the back with overlapping aprons in the front -- and are often called kilted skirts because of this. They can vary in length with hems reaching anywhere from mid calf or ankle length, to lying about mid thigh. The longer variety are often called "Hostess skirts", though tartan skirts cut to a similar length can be done in a variety of modern styles. Often these modern skirts are gathered around the sides and not pleated. They can have much less fabric than a kilt and can also be cut straight or on the bias, and as said above may be pleated or gathered in a variety of styles.

Women's tartan skirts are also more restricted to day wear and morning dress, while standard dresses and gowns made in tartan and often worn with or without tartan sashes are more commonly associated with more formal wear. These will be covered in later corresponding chapters, and information on the appropriate manner of wearing a tartan sash can be found in Appendix E.

Trews

Trews are another common item. They are essentially trousers with a wider waistband and a fishtail back, made of course out of tartan. Anything (shirts, jackets, waistcoats, doublets, etc.) that would normally be worn with a kilt (excluding sporrans) may be worn with trews. Trews are a good alternative to the kilt, especially in the colder months of the year, and are useful for those who simply wish to have something else in tartan as a part of their wardrobe. Trews are just as traditional as kilts and are, (though many see them as a Lowland garment,) in fact considered a part of Highland dress. The distinction between the kilt and trews as a Highland-Lowland divide seems to be yet another one of those instances where romanticism and cultural memory has gotten in the way of truth. Trews are a part of the Scottish National Dress and are just another way of showing one's pride in his tartan. Below you can see an image of trews being worn as day wear.

A good pair of trews will cost about the same as a five-yard kilt, depending of course on the fabric and maker. They are normally high-waisted and can be cut with a fishtail back (as old military officers' trousers were cut) for use with braces or a standard flat cut like suit pants. They are often tapered rather than straight-cut at the leg and are normally worn with some form of ankle boot such as the Chelsea or George when worn as part of an evening wear outfit. Trews can usually be made by most Saxon wear tailors as long as the fabric is provided.

When selecting fabric for trews, a lighter weight wool (around 13 oz.) in a smaller sett is a great option, as 16 oz. or higher fabric can be very heavy and warm, while large-sett tartans may not fully show and may need to be cut down through the main pattern when being used to construct trews.

Trews with a Daywear Ensemble

Sporrans and Other Accessories

From colored hose to sporrans to ties, there are plenty of accessories to THCD that can help you achieve the look you want. I often find that the hardest part of choosing accessories, for those who are new to Highland dress, is getting over engrained Saxon conventions of dress, specifically matching. We often have it in our heads that our outfits must "match", and as I elaborate further in later chapters, that goes out the window when it comes to THCD. Consider day wear, where a man may wear a kilt that is predominantly red in hue but also wears a green tweed jacket with a tattersall shirt, a striped regimental tie, mustard (or another vibrant color) hose, a brown leather day sporran, and black Oxfords! In the conventions of Saxon wear, this would be a sartorial train wreck, but in THCD matching is not a worry. That is not to say you want to build your outfit to be exaggerated or overly vibrant, but not everything needs to match exactly. There is a delicate balance to be had, but this is not as daunting as it sounds. As you try more and more outfits you will learn what works for you and what colors or styles you find pleasing. Accessories are how we build individual character and flavor in our clothing, so it is important to look at what you have or what you would like to achieve, and to experiment with different styles until you get the look you want. This chapter will be broken down into sections covering the various forms of accessories, and each will have a description of the items and explain their usage. The photos in this chapter will highlight a few selected items, and as throughout this book, there are a great variety of accessories in the photos of other chapters in their corresponding levels of dress.

Ties

Ties can be most any form of necktie or bowtie, though the former is the most common. The most common types of ties worn in THCD are generic patterned silk ties and striped regimental or organization ties. Patterned ties, especially those with wild game, national or club symbols, simple patterns, or heraldic designs (including perhaps, your own arms!) are a nice option as well.

Black neck ties, while common in modern Saxon wear, are normally avoided in Highland day wear and morning dress, as they are most often seen at funerals as a sign of mourning. The use of a black necktie for Black Tie or Semi-formal wear should be avoided (when a Bow tie should be worn instead).

Sporrans

Sporrans, of which there are a myriad of styles and designs for purchase, have both functional and decorative elements. Day wear sporrans are usually leather (either buff or suede), can be either plain or embossed, may have tassels, and may have a metal cantle. Day wear sporrans have the most variety as there are many variations of a few standard patterns. I would break them down into plain day sporrans, where they are of a simple all-leather pattern with optional tassels or embossing; hunting sporrans, which have a distinct style, being mostly leather with brass studs throughout; and brass-cantle sporrans. These brass-cantle sporrans are often of the Coronation pattern (often called Ministry of Defence/M.O.D.), or Culloden pattern (also called "Jacobite"), but can also be another form of bespoke style cantle. These normally have brass or sometimes silver-tone cantles (though silver cantles are normally paired with darker colored bags and are often also used in formal sporrans); they may or may not be functional (i.e. have a two piece cantle that opens like a coin purse) and have a myriad of designs. However, they are generally half moon or trapezoidal in shape.

Formal wear sporrans can be very ornate and beautiful. The most common form for many years was the horse hair sporran; the hair usually dyed white with tassels in black; though other color combinations making use of gray and brown are also prevalent. These came in many variations and can still be found in many shops today. The most common taking shape as a long, white-haired sporran with two or three long tassels, and having a simple rolled silver cantle to hold everything in place, though options with more ornate cantles and tassel arrangements can be found also, and some may even have no tassels.

There are some who say that the hair sporran is reserved only for the military or for pipers, and therefore not fit for civilian dress. This is nonsense, as many sporran makers across Scotland and the rest of the world, make civilian hair sporrans that can be customized in many ways. It would, however, be advisable to not wear the uniform sporran of a regiment you haven't served in, or have no family connections to. But to state that all hair sporrans are "off limits" due to their usage by military units or bands is simply wrong.

Common fur sporrans exist in both the full-mask variety and the standard egg shape with a silver cantle. These dress sporrans usually have some form of tassels, either of matching or contrasting fur. Fur sporrans have been made from a variety of furs, most notably seal, fox, rabbit, otter, muskrat, beaver, and badger; and should be reserved for formal wear. In recent years many manufactures have begun using dyed bovine fur as an alternative to seal, either to cut costs or circumvent anti-fur laws. Fur sporrans of the full mask variety have a unique place in THCD, as they have been used for the more formal end of day wear. In fact, I would go so far as to say that full mask sporrans may be used in any level of formality besides casual wear and white tie.

There are also forms of the hair sporran made from the pelts of other animals, most notably that of a goat, which normally do not have tassels. There are also some sporrans that have become popular in recent years that are made from the pelts of Highland cows in a manner similar to goat hair sporrans, as well as the unique one-offs made from the hides of African animals and other big game, and even sporrans made of feathers. While certainly unique, I will leave the opinion on these pieces up to the reader. Just know that when commissioning such an item – regardless of how exotic it is – it is best to find an experienced sporran maker.

A selection of Day and Evening Wear Sporrans

E. L. Roberts-MacDonald

A selection of Metal Cantled Evening Sporrans and one Day Sporran of the MOD Variety

In the past some have asked whether or not hair sporrans are permissible with day wear. Some are vehemently opposed to this, but I would say it depends on the style of sporran. Sporrans with a leather cantle and darker horse hair have been worn at some formal gatherings and are seen in photos going back to the Victorian era. These, in my opinion, are great for morning dress or even day wear under special circumstances. Though, I do not believe that an average Highland games would provide sufficient reason to wear it. If there were a special ceremony happening, or maybe some form of formal clan gathering, then it possibly could be worn. The hair sporran with day wear is an anachronism to be sure, but a welcome one in these modern times, and should you choose to, you will just have to wear it with confidence and pride, as one should with any outfit, be it Saxon or Highland.

There is room for customisation within the world of sporrans. Specially decorated cantles can be cast or carved by most sporran makers. Beyond the simple customisation in geometric or artistic decoration, one can add their own crest or arms to a sporran. Many sporrans with metal cantles also will come with plain spots to have that kind of engraving done.

Hose

Hose for daywear come in many varieties, though they are usually in one solid color and can be found in a variety of knit patterns and colors. White and black hose are often considered to be a faux pas in the traditional community; and after their time as a trend from the 1980s forward, are seemingly becoming less popular. Because of this, I would strongly advise against wearing black or white hose. The other common day wear option is the shooting sock which is like the standard kilt hose in near every way. They are usually thicker and may have a two-color pattern at the hose top in a checkerboard or other stylized pattern. These were originally meant to be worn with tweed breeches while shooting, hence the name. Either form of hose are appropriate for casual, day wear, and morning dress.

Hose

Hose for evening wear can be rather fanciful and beautiful, with the common varieties being Diced hose and Argyll hose. Diced hose are two colors in a checkerboard pattern knitted on the bias. The oldest color scheme, dating back to the 18th century, is red-white. These hose can be worn with any tartan and are seen as a common go to for formal events. Other common color pairings for diced hose include black-red, blue-red, green-red, and blue-green. The general rule of thumb is to match the colors of dicing to one of the colors in the tartan being worn. Argyll hose, sometimes also called tartan hose, are similar to men's Argyll dress socks in pattern, as they are woven in colors matching a certain tartan or set of colors found in a few tartans. You will often see a blue-green-black, or blue-green-gold, hose old as "ancient" colors hose, as either of those colors would match a variety of tartans.

Argyll hose matching a specific tartan usually need to be custom knitted as they are usually complicated patterns mimicking the tartan itself, and are not usually found in most kilt shops.

Hose are normally held up with garter ties, a length of woven wool tape around 32"-36" long and about an inch or so wide; they will also be frayed or fringed at the ends. These are tied around the calf, below the knee, then the hose top is folded over so as to cover the knot and let the tassels hang out on the outside of each leg. Many like to shorten or tuck the ends of the ties so that only a small amount of fringe is seen protruding from the hose top. There are two main knots used, the simple square knot or the older "garter knot" (which is the same as the

Half-Windsor tie knot). which makes one end shorter than the other so the tassels or fringes appear to be stacked. Garter ties can be any color but are often red or some shade of blue. Consider contrasting the color of the garter tie with the color of your hose.

Flashes have been around for some time. Traditional flashes are normally only red and pre-made, with an elastic band and clasp to hold them in place. Their use is rather common in Highland regiments. In recent years, the tartan flashes have gained popularity also, these are made with the scraps of fabric left over from kilt making and attached with an elastic and Velcro strap. They are best avoided; as they have never been used by traditionalists and are often seen as a gimmick of the kilt rental companies or simply a project made from scrap.

A Sgian Dubh tucked into the Hose

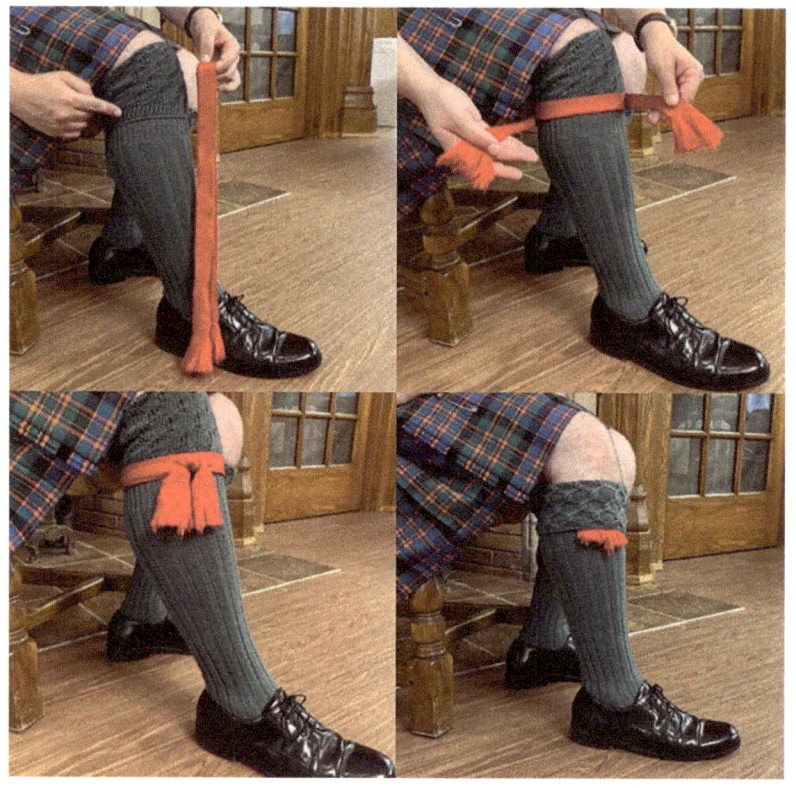

The steps of tying Garter Ties:
1. Locating the fold over line, where the hosetop and hose meet,
2. Taking the tie in half and centering it
at the 2 o'clock position wrapping it once around the leg,
3. Tying the knot and adjusting the tassels,
4. Folding over and adjusting the hose.

Footwear

Footwear in the Highland dress of the past 100 years has been very much the same as that of Saxon wear. The standard shoe is the brogue, which outside of Scotland is usually called an Oxford. Cap-Toes, Wingtips, and Derbies are all common and acceptable choices as well. Another common option is that of the loafer, which is a similar style leather shoe in a slip-on variety. Both Oxfords and loafers can also be called "kilties," meaning that on the top of the shoe there is a leather panel or flap that is fringed to keep dirt and twigs out of the lacing and the top of the shoe. This is either an added flap or an extension of the tongue of the shoe itself.

Ghillie Brogues are often sold as THE shoe for kilt wearing, but these are more common in pipe bands than anywhere else today; and while they are acceptable for day wear, they often sacrifice comfort for the sake of decoration, as the lacing up the leg can cut into the shin and calf. It is rare to see a Scotsman (other than one in Pipe Band or Regimental dress) wearing Ghillie Brogues. The original brogue as worn in the 18th century and earlier was much more akin to a modern hiking sandal or moccasin; it was a function over anything else item, and the kilt industry's use of a so-called modern and traditional equivalent has fallen short.

As mentioned in other chapters the Saxon convention of matching leather colors is not found in Highland dress. The go to color for shoes till the mid 20th century was black, and black shoes can be worn with any color sporran or belt if one chooses. This is not to say that one can't match leathers, as that is simply a matter of personal taste, but if you see someone out and about in black shoes with a brown sporran, do not assume they are out of order.

Sgian

A variety of Day and Dress Sgian Dubh

The Sgian Dubh, also known as the "the wee blade" or "dark blade" is a small fixed blade knife tucked into the hose top for decoration as well as function. The blade length is usually about three to four-inches, with an overall length of around 6 inches, and these can be made as a functional or decorative knife. Often the sgian that one can buy from a kilt shop will have a blunted blade or a plastic handle epoxied into a sheath. These so-called "safety sgian," are a useful tool today as there may be laws in your area that prevent the wearing of a "concealed" knife. The best course of action is to research your local ordinances and go from there. This is also important when traveling abroad.

Sgian can be made for day or evening wear, with the handles of day sgian usually being of horn, antler, or a stained wood. These also normally have brass furnishings. Sgian for formal wear will usually have a black wood or bone with silver furnishings, and possibly the addition of semi-precious stones set into the ferrules or pommel (a Cairngorm stone, for instance, is a traditional choice). A dress sgian could be worn in day wear but if you do this you should try to match it to your metals and or leather being worn with that ensemble. A bone or antler sgian is a good choice for going between day and evening wear. Custom sgian are quite common and any knifemaker should be able to create something unique for you. The all metal sgian that are commonly found online should be avoided however, as they are often rather cheap in construction and lack the classic elegance of a true Highland knife.

Dirks

A 19th century Officer's Dirk from the Crimean War

The Dirk is the largest of the highland knives, and in many ways is the modern long knife, bollock dagger, or even seax of the highlander. While today mostly worn for ceremonial or very formal occasions, the use of the dirk as an accent piece like the sgian dubh is still common.

Dirks are roughly 10-14 inches in length from pommel to tip, with real or decorative blades, and handles of wood, bone, or horn. Dirks worn with day wear should be of wood, bone, or antler handle; and normally have brass fittings on both the blade itself and its matching sheath (which can also be of plain or embossed leather). Formal wear dirks often have bone or black wood handles with silver fittings. Many will also have decorative stones like formal sgian dubhs and may have a small knife and fork that fit into the scabbard.

The dirk can be worn in two different ways. Off a standard wide kilt belt it should be suspended on the side of your dominant hand (like the sgian dubh), and should be worn in plain view. If you are wearing a formal doublet that is worn closed (such as a Balmoral), then simply wear it off the belt in the above manner. In day wear settings, this works better if no waistcoat is being worn. If you are wearing a waistcoat, then you may wear your belt and dirk over the waistcoat. This can be done in a formal setting as well but some low gorge formal waistcoats may not be wide enough for it. If this is the case, or, if you are in day wear with a waistcoat but do not wish to wear a belt simply wear a standard mens belt over the kilt to suspend the dirk, then put on your waistcoat over the belt. Standard dirk sheaths and scabbards will have a roughly 4-6 inch long loop for attachment so that your dirk will hang properly below the waistcoat while concealing the belt.

Pins and Brooches

Pins and brooches are common accessories with Highland attire in both men's and women's wear. In men's wear, the most common of these is the kilt pin, which affixes to the apron for decoration, not function. It is a common myth that the kilt pin is made to hold down the apron from the breeze (or that you even need one), this is false. It is a completely optional piece of decoration; that being said most traditionalists who wear one tend to keep them on the conservative side. A simple large safety pin style kilt pin is all one needs in day wear, and these can be found at any fabric store listed as a kilt/skirt pin, and will only set you back a few dollars or pounds for a pack of two or three. These can also be worn on a long lady's tartan skirt, or in a pinch, can be used to help secure a plaid around your shoulders on a windy day. Formal kilt pins have been made since Victorian times and can be quite beautiful. A Grouse foot kilt pin is still common, as are miniature dirks or swords made of cast silver or other metals, and can be adorned with semi-precious stones. Another option is to wear a clansman badge as a kilt pin with formal wear or in a setting where headgear would not be appropriate, such as in the ballroom or at the dinner table.

A common point of contention among kilt wearers is the proper placement of the kilt pin. This has evolved over time as many things have. Looking at photographs dating from the 1910s till about the 1970s, you see most kilt pins worn about halfway up the apron, as this was the regulation placement in many Highland regiments. I would say that wearing it somewhere between a third to half of the way up the apron would be most appropriate. On a woman's kilted skirt, I would say half way up is the best placement, as it will compliment the longer or shorter nature of those garments respectively.

The next common pin seen with menswear is the lapel pin, which should only be worn on the left-hand side lapel of a day wear jacket. The wearing of a lapel pin on the apron of the kilt, on the hat next to a badge, or in a formal setting is wrong and should be avoided. The wearing of multiple lapel pins is also ill advised, and you will find that wearing a single pin lends itself to a less cluttered look. Two smaller pins may work if they are related to an activity or event, but often less is more.

A selection of Kilt Pins

Lastly, we shall look at the plaid brooch, which is a nice decoration in certain situations. Brooches are mostly used in formal settings, by both men and women, to secure plaids or sashes to the shoulder. The use of a brooch by a man for a day plaid is ill advised, as day plaids are meant to be thrown off the shoulder and to be fairly accessible, thus the wearing of a brooch would only complicate this process. Brooches for men are normally circular or oval shaped, with a variety of patterns and designs cast or engraved into it. Men's brooches are normally about four or five inches in width, with women's brooches being in the two to four inch range. In choosing accessories you can make your outfit both creative and personalized; you can set yourself apart by your fashion choices. One accessory that I mentioned several times but did not elaborate on is that of the plaid, which I thought was so unique in and of itself that it merits its own chapter in this book. As with everything, wear it with confidence and you will be happy.

Determining What to Wear based on the Occasion

I was always told that after six o'clock it was time for black tie. While that convention of dress is not so heavily enforced today, it lends itself to an important truth: the traditional conventions and etiquette of fashion have heavily changed in the past 50 or so years. It used to be that the everyday wear of the common man was a suit of tweed, or similar fabric, and a tie. Presently, if someone was wearing a suit and tie, we'd assume they were a businessman or someone working in a professional setting. For Highland wear this poses a two-fold issue. Firstly, we assume that casual Highland dress is something simple, yet casual dress in the golden age of Highland dress was in fact a kilt, waistcoat, jacket, tie, hose, etc., things we would consider by modern standards to be dressed up; just as what we think of today as formal would not pass in most circles who wear formal dress often. Second, we try to apply the terms used for current business and social fashion as used in Saxon (English/American/Non-Highland) dress; terms like business casual, professional, formal, etc.

that do not fit with the definitions of Highland dress. There is a very delicate balance one must achieve as to not be over or under dressed for an event —thankfully most daytime aspects of Highland wear are lenient on these matters. So, on the following pages I will include a short list of activities and events where the different forms of dress may be appropriate. Keep in mind that some events, such as weddings, may request different forms of dress than as normally accepted. So as always, take everything case by case, read your invitation, or simply ask the organizer.

Day Wear:

Casual:

Anytime casual wear is appropriate, a day out, a hotter day, informal settings.

Outdoor/Sporting wear:

When engaging in activities such as hiking, shooting, or fishing.

Day wear: (Equal to a Business Suit)

Highland games and gatherings, Church, picnics, etc.

Smart day wear: (Morning dress)

Weddings, funerals, garden parties, official functions before 6:00 PM, can also be carried into the evening.

Evening wear:

Black Tie: (Semi- Formal)
Dinner parties, Cocktail parties, dances and balls.

White Tie: (Formal)
Formal balls and galas.

Court Dress:
Seldom used, only at certain functions such as the Coronation of a Sovereign or other special Royal events.

Casual Wear

The idea of "casual" Highland wear is somewhat new, and is mainly due to the fact (and as I discussed in the previous chapter) that casual Highland wear and day wear have always been one in the same. So to create a modern yet traditionally inspired casual wear we have to dip slightly into modern fashion. The idea of a traditionally inspired casual outfit is built upon the idea of casual and day wear being very similar if not the same. With the outfits shown on the next several pages, we see how easily the style can be made into full day wear with the addition of a jacket and tie.

The basic outfit is of course a kilt, hose, day sporran, and some form of simple collared shirt. The shirt either being a simple button down with rolled up sleeves, a short-sleeved button down, or even a polo. These can be made of cotton, poplin, or of some blend, either in a plain color or patterned fabric. A tattersall shirt can also be used for this, I would however avoid using a white or lightly colored 'dress shirt' as this will make the outfit look more like dressed down daywear then a wholly casual set. Further when choosing plain shirts over patterned, try a work shirt or something of a more durable material. These often are of plain twill weave and may have two buttoned pockets on the breast, making this setup great for outdoor activities such as hiking. The next several pages show the basics of a casual day wear outfit in various forms.

E. L. Roberts-MacDonald

Casual Day Wear

Highland Dress: A Comprehensive Illustrated Guide

Casual Day Wear with Cardigan, a normal Pullover Jumper/ Sweater can be used also

E. L. Roberts-MacDonald

The same outfit but with the addition of an Argyll Jacket

As you can see, each outfit also shows aspects of traditional and modern wear. The first shows a more traditional, plain daywear sporran alongside colored hose and oxford shoes, next the same outfit but with the addition of a cardigan. More casual shoes could be worn here also, such as tassel loafers, slip ons, or even a basic leather ankle boot or chukar. A belt would also be a nice touch, but it is not needed to hold up the kilt as said in previous chapters. It would simply be a fashion accessory. Other possible additions would be a simple pull over sweater or a cardigan; if one was looking for warmth in the spring or autumn months. This same outfit can of course be upgraded to full daywear with the inclusion of a tie and jacket. Or simply, the jacket over the sweater. That is often done with fairisle sweater vests however (which can be worn by themselves without a jacket in a casual setting, with or without a tie).

In casual wear, layering is your friend. The versatility of it is perfect. It serves its purpose on hot days or cool ones; or when you wish to be kilted around the home or out for an easy afternoon walk. All and all I find this style to be my go-to for everyday wear.

Casual Wear for the Ladies

For women, casual and daywear are more blended. Here the outfit may be of a simpler style, as will be shown in the chapter on day wear, consisting of a tartan skirt and blouse with more comfortable, rather than dressier shoes. Like menswear women could wear a sweater or cardigan in cooler temperatures, and could also wear a ladies tweed blazer and scarf.

E. L. Roberts-MacDonald

*Simple summer Casual Wear
for the Ladies*

VII

Daywear

When people think of Traditional Highland Dress they usually conjure up in their mind the classic tartan and tweed daywear ensemble. Daywear is truly fascinating and unique as it can take many different forms. It also leaves the perfect amount of creative room so as to create a rather unique look. The base items of men's Highland daywear are: the kilt, shirt (plain, check, or tattersall), tie, jacket (usually of tweed), waistcoat (an optional piece, but usually in tweed or tartan), colored kilt hose or shooting socks, brogues (usually a plain or brogued oxford), sporran, and then other accessories, which have their own dedicated chapters.

Day wear is also quite versatile, as the traditional Saxon convention of matching fabrics is not needed in Highland dress; meaning it is perfectly acceptable to wear a patterned tattersall shirt, tartan kilt, and a striped tie. This also means that you may wear "loud" tweeds with heavy patterns, as was common back in the golden age of THCD. You may contrast your kilt and tweed options, you may wear a waistcoat and jacket of two different tweeds, or you may even choose to wear a waistcoat of the same tartan as your kilt! Looking at photos from the 1920s-60s you will see the mixing of certain items that are not of the same level of dress or even time period worn as well. Things such as antique sporrans of leather, fur, and hair, as well as belts worn over the waistcoat to suspend a dirk (a Victorian holdover), while these outfits are not entirely vintage, the inclusion of these heirloom pieces adds character to the overall appearance of an outfit. On the following pages you will see photos of several gentlemen arrayed in various forms of Highland day wear.

Highland Dress: A Comprehensive Illustrated Guide

Daywear with a matching tweed Jacket and Waistcoat

E. L. Roberts-MacDonald

*Daywear with a tweed Jacket and
Fairisle sweater vest*

*Daywear with Barathea Wool Jacket,
Belt, & Day Plaid*

E. L. Roberts-MacDonald

Daywear with matching guncheck tweed Jacket & Waistcoat

Highland Dress: A Comprehensive Illustrated Guide

Daywear with tweed Jacket and Day Plaid, without Belt

As you can see these photos show a great variety of styles, some with solid tweeds, some contrasting with the kilt, and some matching, some with or without waistcoats, one even including a sweater vest (a common addition, can be plain or of a fair isle variety), some with shooting socks and some with kilt hose.

You may also notice that there are a variety of jacket cuts presented as well. The main forms being the Crail (which is most akin to a Saxon cut blazer, with straight cuffs and buttons), the Argyll (which has gauntlet cuffs and scalloped pocket flaps), and the Braemar (which will have a cuff similar to that of a Prince Charlie coatee and may have straight or scalloped pocket flaps); there are also a variety of bespoke jackets that do not fall under any one style, these can still be seen today.

A variety of patterned Tweed Jackets

Three Jacket Cuffs: two Gauntlet, one with antler buttons and the other with leather covered buttons, and a two button Crail cuff

All of these jackets may or may not have epaulets at the shoulders, as these are a matter of personal preference. It should also be noted that a traditional Saxon cut tweed jacket should never be worn with the kilt as it is cut far longer than a kilt jacket. As discussed in prior chapters, the kilt in day wear may of course be substituted for trews if you desire, as this is a completely acceptable and traditional choice. You may also wear a regular tweed kilt jacket with trews or a Saxon cut jacket, as displayed on the next page. They can also be worn in conjunction with a tartan waistcoat. When wearing trews, I find that the most common footwear choice in day wear would be the brogue or a simpler leather boot, while Chelsea and George boots are common for formal wear. Either option would be appropriate.

Women's daywear has often been a hard area to establish conventions, mainly from the fact that women's fashion changes at a much faster rate than mens fashion. As discussed previously, the kilted skirt and other tartan skirts are the main item with which convention is assigned, creating an interesting dichotomy. From here, do women take their fashion queues from the men, or do they simply add tartan into the existing fashion? I am apt to agree with the latter choice, as that has seemed to be the general course of women's Highland wear for the past two hundred years. Sashes were added to existing dresses and gowns, tartan shawls worn over standard clothes, and new dresses and gowns made from silk woven tartan.

So, if we are to take to the idea of women's Highland wear being standard women's fashion with a splash of tartan thrown in we get the next few examples. A gathered tartan skirt cut on the bias with a blouse, and possibly a womans jacket or blazer. This could be of a standard fashion fabric, or could be of tartan or tweed. As day wear is somewhat dressy, I feel this is also the more appropriate time to use the longer gathered skirt or longer hostess skirt, as they are the dressier option, with the short kilted skirts being more casual.

Sashes could also be worn here, as could more subtle flashes of tartan, such as rosettes bearing a smaller clansman's badge or brooch, or possibly a tartan scarf worn around the neck. My advice on ladies Highland wear is to have fun, be unique, and add your splashes of tartan where you would like.

Ladies Daywear with Tartan Skirt, Blouse, and a Dancing Sash.

Highland Dress for the Sportsman and Hiker

Scotland is a rugged and beautiful country, with many having described it as a sportsman's paradise. This is, of course, apparent if one looks at the massive industries fueled by hiking, hunting, fishing, camping, and other outdoor activities in the country. As such, many aspects of THCD have evolved to fit the needs and demands of the terrain and climate, but in recent years many have said that enjoying these recreational pastimes while in Highland dress is near impossible due to the so-called "dressy" nature of our national dress. This chapter will hopefully elaborate on the various ways you can dress for the great outdoors in a Highland manner.

The issue with fitting the Highland outdoor styles of the past into the modern world is similar to that discussed in our chapter on casual wear, that being that as a society, what was considered casual is now considered "dressed up," and as fashion in both the regular and outdoor world has evolved many modern sportsmen and hikers have branded the old styles and equipment as obsolete. That sentiment could not be farther from the truth. Throughout this brief chapter you will probably notice many overlaps with casual and day wear

Highland dress; this chapter merely exists to explain and suggest items that would be acceptable to participate in many outdoor activities while maintaining traditional Highland dress. And this chapter's placement after casual and day wear will be made more apparent in time, as you see their influences here.

Footwear

As an experienced hiker and outdoorsman, I will confidently say one of the most important items in any hiker or outdoorsman's arsenal is a good boot. You can't rightly walk anywhere without a sturdy pair! So, you might as well invest in a good pair that fits well and will last you a long time. The historic footwear of the Highlander going back into the 18th, and in some respects 19th centuries, was the ghillie brogue, a sort of moccasin which, as explained in previous chapters, is very different from the modern shoe sold by many vendors today. It was an item of necessity and not one of fashion or recreation.

The term Ghillie Brogue has been used too to describe a shoe commonly worn by (you guessed it) ghillies in the mid to late 19th century. A crossover of the sturdy, everyday shoes of that era and the older more moccasin-like item of the previous century. These often were of thick soles, hobnailed, and also fitted with the kiltie flaps described in the footwear section of the earlier chapter on accessories; these also would have had actual holes for drainage, leading them to look somewhat more like the modern shoe of the same name. When modern hiking and camping became popular in the early 1900s, the choice of footwear for outdoorsmen then, and still today, became the ankle boot. These are mainly made of leather with natural or modern soles and provide firm support around the ankle and are waterproof in most cases. Important qualities in rugged Highland terrain.

Boots should be worn with normal wool kilt hose, which are heavy and padded, making them a great hiking sock. If you need another layer, a pair of regular ankle or crew socks can be worn over the hose and turned down over the top of the boot, this can provide extra padding, support, and warmth. This also has a wicking effect, pulling sweat away from the wool hose and into the other sock, allowing for the outer sock to be changed more frequently instead of having to constantly change kilt hose. Another common piece of footwear is the Wellington boot, which is either made of leather or a synthetic material, and is about calf or knee high. These are especially useful in boggy and wet terrain. I would not recommend them for extended hiking, however for shorter walks or shooting these may be a better option, as they provide more protection to the exposed kilt hose. When not wearing a tall boot, gaiters and or puttees are a great asset, especially when it is cold or you are passing through underbrush or thickets.

In the case of shirts for hiking, a button down in a cotton or poplin fabric is the preferred choice in warm weather. This can be either long or short sleeved. In cooler weather, a simple solid color flannel is a good choice, as would a wool or heavier cotton shirt. Here you can see the standard kilt, button down, hose (worn with an extra sock), and boot. Other accessories include a canvas hiking pack, walking stick, and a simple day sporran.

E. L. Roberts-MacDonald

Casual Highland wear for Hiking

In cooler weather a sweater or an outdoor jacket could be added as well. The Barbour and similar styles are quite common with the hikers and sportsmen of Scotland, as are modern synthetic rain coats; as well as boxier shirt-jacs made of flannel, wool, or waxed canvas, and are quite comfortable. Since these are outerwear jackets, their length is not as standard, so don't be alarmed if the jacket comes down a little farther than a regular kilt jacket.

On the topic of jackets, there is a less common, but still very traditional style of jacket similar to the Saxon wear tweed shooting or Norfolk jacket. These can be cut in many ways, but some general characteristics include deep pockets in the front for shells, a high set of external pockets for a watch or flask, a gusset or pair of gussets at the back either down the center seam or at the shoulders, and then an optional quilted shoulder pad. An example can be found here, cut more like an argyll jacket with a shorter cutaway, quilted shoulder pad, and scalloped pockets with matching gauntlet cuffs.

These jackets are also lined, giving the wearer more protection from the cold than the standard suiting weight tweed. You can see in the photo that the subject is wearing a standard set of hose and ankle boots, as well as a day sporran.

E. L. Roberts-MacDonald

A Kilt-cut Shooting Jacket

These jackets are usually closed in the front, and are worn on a level closer to day wear with either a plain or check shirt as well as a tie. In situations like this I find that a woolen tie and thicker shirt are often welcome as the tie seals the shirt around the neck protecting you from the elements.

The last item one should consider obtaining or making is the highland form of walking stick, often called a Cromach, Cromag, or crook. These walking sticks provide extra support when traversing hills or fording streams. The top of the stick may be decorated in many ways, either being bent into a crook, finished with a pronged antler, or finished with a carved and polished horn. The true Highland stick should come to the armpit and be at least one to two inches in diameter. Other shorter variants such as the market stick, which are between waist and chest height and finished in a similar fashion may also be acceptable.

In closing, Highland sporting wear, while similar to that of casual and day wear, can be useful in any manner of situations, with some of these activities coming back into fashion and the recent trend of vintage and vintage inspired hiking and camping hopefully this has helped shed a little light on the subject.

Morning Dress or "Smart Daywear"

Morning dress is an interesting topic in regard to Highland wear, mostly due to the fact that, in the United Kingdom, if an event required morning dress, the standard Saxon wear equivalent is preferred. However, as of late there has evolved a Highland equivalent of morning dress, one that combines elements from both day wear and formal wear. First though, we should define what morning dress is. Usually, it is seen as "formal day wear," similar to what is worn at weddings or fancy garden parties. It is also worn for any royal event before six o'clock PM. If morning dress is requested, it should be specified by the event host. Morning dress should not be confused with "semi- formal", as the Saxon equivalent to that is black tie. The versatility of this dress code often lends itself well to private pipers at weddings and funerals, as it is not a uniform, nor is it too casual or too formal for most settings where a piper would be requested to play.

E. L. Roberts-MacDonald

    The standard Highland form of morning dress is built upon the basic day wear ensemble: Kilt, jacket (usually an Argyll of black or another dark color baratheа wool), waistcoat (either matching the jacket or tartan), hose of a darker color such as claret or navy (avoid black), black oxfords, and a sporran. The jacket may also be of tweed, but when using a tweed jacket for morning dress it is wise to stick to a more conservative fabric; something like a gun check or houndstooth would likely be too loud for occasions calling for morning dress. You could also of course wear trews instead of a kilt, hose, and sporran. When selecting a sporran for morning dress, avoid the so-called "semi-formal" sporran. They are not traditional nor will you see Scottish traditionalists wearing them. Any formal or dark leather sporran would be appropriate, as would fur or horse hair. The full mask sporran lends itself greatly here, as it truly can be worn in any day wear, morning dress, or black tie ensemble. When it comes to ties it is a safe bet to stick to something conservative, solid or possibly a dark stripe. Regimental, university, or society ties would also be appropriate, but I would avoid anything that would be considered flashy.

    Here you can see a variety of morning dress with both kilts and trews. Also a variety of jackets, sporrans, and other accouterments. A general rule of thumb in regard to morning dress is to save it for weddings and funerals, if it is requested by the host or organizer for another form of event, then it would be of course appropriate, but otherwise I would stick to day wear for the bulk of daytime events.

Highland Morning Dress with black Argyll Jacket, Tartan Waistcoat, Diced Hose, & Formal Sporran

E. L. Roberts-MacDonald

Highland Morning Dress with Charcoal Tweed Jacket & Waistcoat, with a full mask Sporran

Highland Morning Dress with Black Argyll, and tartan Trews & Waistcoat

Eveningwear, Black Tie and White Tie

The most beautiful form of Highland dress can be found in the ballroom. Dancers stepping to the tune of the pipes and fiddle; putting on a vast array of tartan, with highlights of fine silverwork; handsomely cut doublets and elegant gowns. Highland evening wear is the perfect time to pull out all the stops and get creative, as there are so many beautiful styles and accouterments to select from when building a formal Highland outfit. And of course, no Highlanders wardrobe would be complete without it!

Highland evening wear can be separated into two main dress codes: Semi-formal wear and Formal wear; more commonly called Black tie and White tie. It seems today that in many places, black tie is the go to for most evening events, which often makes it seen as the common option, as white tie formal will usually only be seen at functions such as balls, galas, and state dinners. It should be noted that while black tie is often considered "formal" it is not "full formal". Highland wear, as always, has a few interesting caveats to it and this is especially true here. For example, in a Saxon wear setting, wearing white tie to a black tie event would make you overdressed (and be a faux pas), whereas with Highland wear wearing something like a lace jabot would not be out of the norm; as a jabot and cuffs could be worn at either as it does not fit the solidified rules of either Saxon white or black tie. It appears more like white tie or court dress, but it sits outwith the common conventions of either, so wearing it as a sort of catch-all would not be considered a faux pas. A perk of Highland wear is that you have several options in terms of jacket or doublet style; and in your accessories, i.e. sporran, hose, etc., that you do not have with Saxon wear. Keep in mind that there are many old and new bespoke jackets and doublets for formal wear that do not fit standardized names, these are also perfectly acceptable options. Bespoke doublets and jackets have always been quite common in traditional Highland wear; oftentimes you will see these in old photos and be perplexed, as an item may seem like an amalgamation of commonly seen styles. If you wish to go the route of a fully custom design, looking through historic photos of formal Highland events would be a great start.

Black Tie

Firstly, we will discuss semi- formal wear, also known as black tie. Highland black tie is so much more than just a kilt, Prince Charlie jacket and waistcoat, a rabbit fur sporran, and plain hose; as was the fashion throughout much of the 1980s and 1990s. It can be quite beautiful if you take the time to collect or invest in nice kit. For the most part the main forms of jacket and waistcoat used in black tie are the Prince Charlie (PC) and the Regulation Doublet (RD). There are many more of course but these are the most common as they most align with Saxon cut dinner and military mess dress jackets. There has also been a recent trend of formal Argyll jackets, cut in black barathea wool and adorned in silver buttons like the Prince Charlie and Regulation Doublet. The Prince Charlie is cut shorter than the normal kilt jacket, usually with straight sleeve cuffs and adorned with buttons on the sleeve, breast, epaulets, and tails. The waistcoat worn with it is usually of a three button, low gorge variety, and can be made of matching fabric to the jacket or in tartan. The Regulation Doublet is much the same, but with the addition of tashes (flaps cut similar to tails) on the sides of the jacket. It should be noted that even though the name Regulation Doublet evokes a somewhat military idea, this is fully a civilian garment that can be worn by anyone.

As said above something like a Lace Jabot and cuffs would be appropriate with black tie when worn with a Sherrifmuir, Balmoral, Montrose, or Kenmore style Doublet. These can, of course, be worn with a black bow tie as well (with exception of the Kenmore and only with the lapels turned back on the Montrose).

Most of these jackets and doublets have a certain style of waistcoat to match; as said above with the Prince Charlie and Regulation Doublet, the main style is a low gorge, three button waistcoat, usually to match the jacket, but tartan options can be made and worn quite well. If wearing an Argyll jacket in a black tie setting you may wear a normal tartan waistcoat, but the buttons should match either the jacket's or be covered in matching tartan fabric.

With black tie one would normally wear a white shirt with an open turn-down collar; a shirt with a wingtip collar would be acceptable but those are more commonly seen with white tie today. The use of long black neck ties with a jacket for semi-formal wear is debated; it may work with a balmoral, Sherrifmuir, or even a Montrose with its lapels folded back, but it is not normally considered Traditional Highland Dress.

You can, of course, wear a kilt or tartan trews with black tie. Both are equally acceptable. When wearing a kilt, for the lower end of black tie solid, darker colored hose may be worn, but it is worth investing in a pair of diced or tartan hose.

Highland Dress: A Comprehensive Illustrated Guide

The Prince Charlie Jacket, note the tail and the absence of tashes. Cuffs are normally of this style (also often called "Prince Charlie") though they may be gauntlet cuffs as well.

E. L. Roberts-MacDonald

The Regulation Doublet, this is a Prince Charlie with side tashes, making it a doublet. This example is shown with gauntlet cuffs.

The Dress Argyll is made of dark (normally black) wool and has silver buttons. It can be worn for less formal Black-Tie affairs with a bowtie but could also be worn with a lace jabot as shown here.

E. L. Roberts-MacDonald

The Kenmore Doublet is normally worn buttoned up and belted; and with a lace jabot. The Montrose is simply a double-breasted Kenmore without tashes. The Balmoral is similar in cut and is worn belted and closed, but has lapels at the neck.

The Sherrifmuir Doublet is somewhere between a Montrose and Regulation Doublet. It is worn with a waistcoat and lace jabot.

E. L. Roberts-MacDonald

Simple Black Tie, with black Argyll, tartan Waistcoat & Hose, and a full mask Sporran

Black Tie with a belted Balmoral Doublet, Fur Sporran, & Tartan Hose

E. L. Roberts-MacDonald

Two Prince Charlie Ensembles: One with a hair Sporran & diced Hose, one with fur Sporran & tartan Hose

Tartan Trews with matching bias cut Waistcoat & Prince Charlie Coatee

Of course, for those interested in true sartorial elegance, you may also consider more traditional accouterments, and local customs. For instance, instead of a ready to wear collared shirt, one might consider a collarless shirt with detachable collar, enabling you to select the most appropriate collar for the occasion (Imperial, High Imperial, Wing, Butterfly wing, Arundel, Albany, Round, Spearpoint, D'orlando, Burlington, etc.) You should also consider the region specific sartorial customs. For example, a gentleman hailing from Perthshire always wears a white bow tie, even to a black tie event.

Women's Formal Highland Wear

Women's highland black tie has some variation. For the lower end of black tie and morning dress, a simple knee length cocktail dress would be perfectly appropriate; accenting this with a tartan sash or rosette, or a tartan fabric belt would round out the outfit perfectly. For the higher end of black tie, a longer dress of a colored fabric, with a full tartan sash and rosette would be most appropriate. A ball gown would also work here, but it may be a better option for white tie. With both levels of formality ladies tartan sashes can be made of either wool woven tartan or silk woven tartan; and can be secured with either a plain silver brooch or something more fancy with pearls or stones set in and matching your jewelry.

Highland Dress: A Comprehensive Illustrated Guide

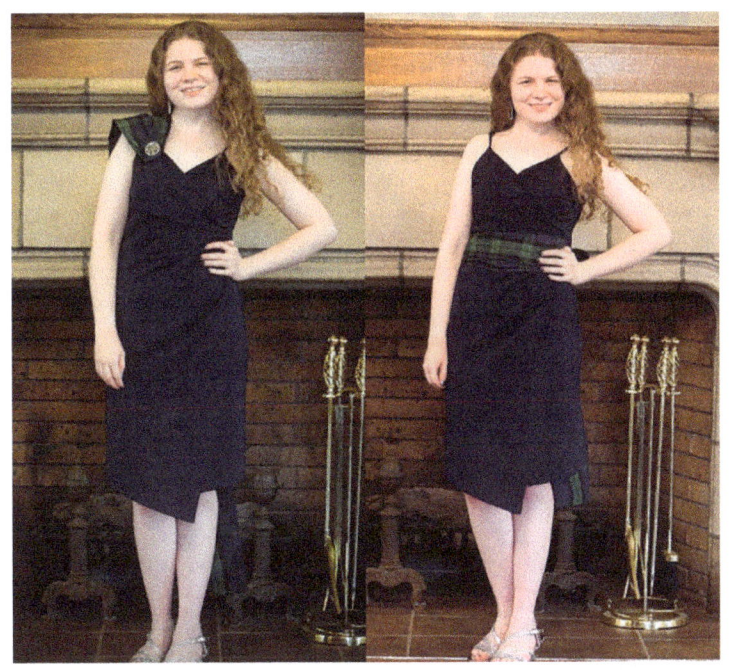

Ladies Black Tie Wear: With Sash pinned for dancing or worn as a belt

A Ladies Sash Buckle on Silk-Tartan Sash

E. L. Roberts-MacDonald

A Ladies Formal Gown with Silk-Tartan Sash

White Tie

Formal wear, more colloquially known as "White Tie" has various expressions in THCD. As said before some forms of evening doublets may be useful and acceptable for both black and white tie events, examples of this include the Sherrifmuir, Balmoral, Kenmore, and Montrose, when worn with a lace jabot and cuffs. The other seldom seen white tie option is the Prince Charlie or Regulation Doublet but worn with a white tie and a white or tartan waistcoat, cut with the same low gorge of the standard Prince Charlie or Regulation Doublet waistcoat.

When it comes to accessories with Highland evening wear there are many options as far as sporrans, hose, footwear, and other accessories. Sporrans should be either full mask, silver or brass cantled fur, or some form of hair, Sporrans have been further elaborated on in the accessories chapter with accompanying photographs. Tartan and diced hose are the all-around best option for black and white tie, and as always one should avoid plain white hose. Tartan hose should match or closely resemble the tartan of the kilt being worn. Diced hose are usually two toned and can either match the main colors of the tartan or can be contrasting, as the photos above show. The original white and red diced hose can go with any outfit, while the tartan hose match the kilt being worn.

The most common footwear for formal dress is the buckled brogue. They are black and bear silver buckles as was common in the 18th and 19th centuries. Black Ghillie brogues can be worn for black tie functions, as well as black oxfords; though these would be out of place in full formal dress. Depending on the event (for example, a dinner where a Royal Patron presides), court pumps may also be appropriate.

Other items that can be worn would be formal belts to be worn over the Balmoral, Kenmore, and Montrose doublets. Wearing a large kilt belt with a Prince Charlie under waistcoat is seen as a faux pas in formal wear, just as it is in day wear. Dirks have also been worn with formal dress. If you wish to wear a dirk while in a low gorge waistcoat, a standard thin belt worn under the waistcoat is an acceptable way to suspend the dirk while avoiding a bulky look under the waistcoat; this trick can also be done with a tall day wear waistcoat as well.

It should be advised, however, that a cross belt and sword are out of place in civilian dress, except in the Scottish Court Dress; which hasn't been seen in nearly seventy years (the last event where it was used being the coronation of H.M. Queen Elizabeth II).

The other common decorations seen with formal wear are military medals and decorations in the forms of miniatures worn on the lapel of the jacket, as well as neck devices and breast stars. Note that full sized medals are never worn with formal attire (although neck medals, breast stars and sashes are).

A full appendix on the conventions of wearing medals and other awards can be found in the back of this book.

The last accoutrement is the plaid, which has a dedicated chapter. I will note here that plaids are not often seen anymore with formal wear, and that the "fly plaid" that is often seen worn in today's kilt hire industry should be avoided at all costs, as it is neither functional, smart, or convenient (especially when dancing or dining); and as there are plenty of other plaid designs that lend themselves better to formal wear in both a sartorial and practical regard.

Headgear

Headgear, in general, has seemed to fall out of favor in recent years in both mens and womens fashion; with Highland dress however, it is still quite common. There are two main forms of headgear in Highland dress: the Balmoral and the Glengarry. There are, of course, variants of the Balmoral (such as the Tam o' Shanter and Kilmarnock), but these are all fairly close and often the names are used interchangeably by many. The Balmoral, and its derivatives, are usually knitted with a round crown similar to a beret. It should be noted that a beret is not THCD and is best avoided entirely. The Kilmarnock is of similar shape, however, the side and top pieces of the hat are normally two separate, sewn together pieces. The crown can either be rather large or about the same size as the band. The Tam o' Shanter is a balmoral with a larger crown, and was standard military issue in Highland regiments for many years. This has led to the term Tam or Tam o' Shanter being used interchangeably with the Balmoral Since.

A Balmoral Bonnet with Dicing

The best comparison for the Glengarry is the Garrison Cap. It is often said that the Glengarry is only for military wear, but a brief examination of photos of Highland wear over the past 125 years would disprove that notion. There is another school of thought that the above statement applies to, many say that Glengarries and even Balmorals that have dicing around the crown are somehow reserved for military usage, which is completely ridiculous when one considers the many commercial and homemade bonnets that bear the bonnets main color diced with white; or again the many historic photos that would disprove this notion as well. Another common source of legend and "tradition" is the positioning of tails on one's hat. There are many who will preach that unwed men let the tails hang untied and that married men tie them in a short bow(I have heard the reverse said as well); this is yet another instance of an "ancient Highland tradition" being absolutely made up. You may wear your tails however you like (or cut them off entirely for that matter).

A plain Glengarry Bonnet

These styles of headgear mostly flourish in the casual and day wear settings of Highland dress, as wearing a hat indoors or at a formal function is generally considered to be a faux pas in both Saxon and Highland conventions. The wearing of headgear does however present an opportunity for you to sport an unique form of identification other than the clan tartan — that is of course the clansman badge.

The simple clansman badge is attached to the cockade of the bonnet and usually depicts the crest of the clan chiefs' personal armorial bearings, which is then surrounded by a strap and buckle usually containing the chiefs' motto or slogan. All clansmen are entitled to wear the badge of their chief; however, it is considered wrong to wear the badges of two different clans at the same time, as this would indicate your splitting allegiances between two different individuals. Badges also exist too for local Scottish societies, games associations, clubs, and other causes, as do plain generic badges containing a saltire, lion rampant, harp, or other national symbols.

The Clansman's Badge for a follower of the Chief of MacPherson

You may sometimes see at a highland games or clan gathering certain individuals wearing special variations of the cap badge, with either small metal or full-sized eagle feathers behind. This is a mark of rank that goes back to the early 1800s and possibly before, and was originally outlined by the planners of Geroge IV's State Visit to Scotland in 1822. It has since condensed into a more rounded system of rank; with changes made over time as our clan system evolves. This system is linked to Heraldry, another system of personal identification going back to the Middle Ages. In Scotland, as well as the rest of the United Kingdom and Commonwealth, heraldry is personal, i.e, there is no such thing as a "family" coat of arms. Individuals may be granted or otherwise legally acquire personal armorial bearings via a heraldic authority or society in regulation with their own country's laws on heraldry — in Scotland, arms are granted by the Lord Lyon, King of Arms. It should be made clear that the wearing of feathers is not regulated as a part of heraldry, indeed there are non-armigers who are entitled via their position within a clan or organization to display feathers, but unless you are an armiger (or person who has been told that you may display such marks of rank within an organization) you should not wear feathers.

The current system is for armigers to wear their own crest, either with or without a circlet, which may contain your motto or slogan, and the appropriate number of feathers based on rank; either in metal or real feathers. The appropriate conventions are as follows and are illustrated for you here:

E. L. Roberts-MacDonald

The Crest Badge of John Wright of Deerfield

The Crest Badge of the Baron of Balvaird

The Crest Badge of the Chief of Clan MacPherson

The Crest Badge of the Sovereign

E. L. Roberts-MacDonald

Armigers wear one feather. Chieftains wear two feathers; these are the heads of cadet branches within a clan as well as the sons of the Chief. Scottish Feudal Barons are also understood to fit within the two feather category, as they are considered to be senior armigers with a following. A full Chief wears three feathers behind his crest, as do the children of the Sovereign. Armigers who are also Peers, or have feudal tenure are entitled to place their proper coronet of rank or cap of maintenance upon the circlet if they so choose (as shown in the two feather variant). The last badge illustrated is that of the Royal Crest as used in Scotland, with four feathers set behind. This is the understood number of feathers for the Sovereign to display (however there was a point when it was suggested that the Sovereign wear five feathers). This badge also shows the crown set upon the circlet as a coronet of rank. The last King to wear four feathers was George IV. Prince Albert(the Consort of Queen Victoria) often wore three (or was posed with a bonnet bearing three in portraits). And in the reigns of George V and George VI, they each only ever wore three. So while precedent shows only three feathers being worn in the past century, the convention is still written for the extra, should a future King or Queen choose to display them.

Additionally those clansfolk who are delegated representatives of a chief, and who are not armigers themselves, and who have their chiefs permission may wear one or two feathers behind the standard clansman's badge. This practice has become common in recent years for the commissioners and heads of various clan societies. This is usually only done at clan events and highland games where the representative is there on behalf of the chief. As said before, the court of Lord Lyon King of Arms does not regulate the wearing of feathers, as its purpose is to maintain the heraldic laws and customs of Scotland. The eagle feathers are marks of rank within the clan system which is separate from the heraldic systems of the world, and its traditions should be respected. The wearing of feathers from other birds is permissible but not advised as one would not want to accidentally be mistaken for a clan officer when they do not hold that position themselves.

For a clansman the best addition to the bonnet besides the clansman badge is the plant badge, a small sprig of a flower or tree that is tucked behind the badge. These add a bit of color and can be worn behind the bonnet badge or a pin. A list of plant badges by clan can be found in Appendix D of this book.

For the ladies, a balmoral would work for headgear; as would any other style of womens hat. Like in the clothing itself, there are few real Highland conventions on ladies headgear. Often the hat is whatever goes best with the existing Highland outfit, perhaps with a cockade, or in the shown example, a tartan ribbon and sprigs of the clan's plant badge tucked in. Women who are armigers could wear a balmoral or similar style hat with their feathers, or may use a silver badge with set silver feathers as a brooch or sash pin. Always feel free to be creative with your wardrobe.

E. L. Roberts-MacDonald

*A Ladies Sun Hat with Tartan Ribbon Bow
gathered around Plant Badges*

The Plaid

The plaid is probably one of the most underrated accessories in Highland dress; many see it as a symbol of status and not one of function. Hopefully in this chapter I can explain the many forms and uses of the plaid. Now, when I speak of a plaid you may have several ideas come to mind, a fly plaid? A drummer's or piper's plaid? A full plaid or laird's plaid? Well the truth is the term "plaid" is applied to several different items in THCD which makes things very confusing. When one refers to a plaid, especially in a day setting, they are referencing the standard day plaid which has many names; the laird's plaid or shepherd's plaid probably being the most common of these names. For the purposes of this chapter, we will refer to it as a day plaid or simply, plaid as that has been the most common name for the item in question throughout history.

The plaid, first and foremost, is an item of functionality. It is an extra layer of fabric to wrap yourself in to protect from wind, and rain, and snow; or it is a picnic blanket to lay out in the field or hillside to rest on for a break. The plaid has barely changed in 400 years, and arguably has been around since ancient times (as it is basically a cloak). In practice, it is just a large piece of heavyweight fabric, the only thing that has really changed in the past few centuries is the choice of material and the ways we wear it. The usefulness of this garment as a cloak or decoration is wonderful, but also quite basic. The plaid can be in the same tartan as the kilt, or in another tartan of the clan (or of a plain check).

When you have a kilt made, look into ordering a few extra yards of fabric to use as a plaid if you would like it to match your kilt. You may also find some yardage of wool that is in another one of your clan's tartans or color schemes, as the plaid and kilt do not have to match (though it should be said that the tartans should be from the same clan). The average measurements of a plaid are somewhere around two to three yards of double width fabric, and at least 16 ounces in weight. Single width is fine if you wish to wrap it around your body like a piper's plaid or wear it folded and gathered on the shoulder, but keep in mind that it will not be wide enough to use as a cloak or blanket. The edges can be left unaltered, though it is most common to see them fringed or purled on the short ends. Below you will find some picture examples of how a plaid may be used or worn with descriptions of how it is gathered or folded.

Probably the most common way to wear a day plaid is to fold it and place it over the left shoulder, fringe down in the front with the main fold in the back. Normally, the front end is worn longer, coming to or just past the hem of the jacket. When folding, fold your plaid in half then in half again lengthwise, then fold in half widthwise. This will leave you with a fold at one end and two fringed ends at the other. The fringes can be aligned or staggered too for flair. This also gives you the base to unfold or use the plaid in the following styles.

The second most common way to wear the plaid is to fold it multiple times lengthwise, as described above, so that it creates a length of fabric about eight or so inches wide, this is then wrapped around the body in a manner similar to a piper's plaid. With one end of it being placed over the left shoulder coming down to somewhere between the breast and the hem of the jacket. The remainder of the plaid is then wrapped around the back of the body, under the right arm, and then over the left shoulder again. The back should lay longer than the front. With this style it is important to remember that a brooch is not normally worn but could be if you so desire. The weight of the plaid should keep it on your shoulder.

E. L. Roberts-MacDonald

The over the left shoulder method

The Plaid worn across the body. A brooch could be added for extra security or flair

The day plaid also has the wonderful function of serving as an extra layer in inclement weather. Here I have folded the plaid in half down its length, then placed it over my shoulders in a fashion much like a shawl or stole. This provides a cape down the back of the jacket nearly three-foot long, as well as protection around the shoulders and down the front. In rain, snow, and wind this is my go-to option for an extra layer of warmth and protection from the elements. You will see pictures and drawings going back hundreds of years showing shawls, blankets, and even day plaids being worn in this manner for these very reasons. The second photo is the same set up but since the plaid is folded in half the extra material from the fold can be brought up over the head like a hood in the foulest of conditions. An extra layer of warmth over the head besides the bonnet is always welcome in the cold. An added bonus is that since these styles are supported by the shoulders, a belt could also be worn over the plaid and around the waist to hold the bottom half to your body, thus freeing your arms.

The final use of the plaid that I will reference here is its use as a ground cloth or picnic blanket. After a long days walk it's a nice way to sit and enjoy lunch or to sit and watch the events at a Highland games with your plaid keeping your Kilt off the ground.

Highland Dress: A Comprehensive Illustrated Guide

Closing Words

Traditional Highland dress is an important part of the identity of both natural Scots and the many millions of men and women around the world who make up the Scottish diaspora. The conventions laid out here are a formula to create a classic and timeless look; most of which are not firm rules. You must be comfortable and confident in your wear, if not, the next generation won't take up the tartan mantle. Be gentle when educating new folks. Be patient, and always take time to learn, study, research, and most of all do not be afraid to ask questions of those who are the everyday experts in the subject, that is to say both the Highland country folk who don the kilt in the homeland, and those who still wear it though they be far from home. This book is meant to be a basic overview of the subject. There are many quirks of local custom and of misunderstood ideas which permeate into the fashion to this day. There are many good resources out there, almost off of which I have used as source material for this book, which you can find in the back. There is also a glossary of terms there and number of appendices. We hope that you find them helpful.

Appendices

Appendix A: A Reference for Dress

This short list of basic items of kit is meant to be a quick guide to what to wear with each level of dress. More information on each is found in the corresponding chapters of this book. Each list is items in addition to the kilt or trews.

Casual:

Shirt: Plain or patterned button down, short or long sleeved.

Hose: Plain color or shooting socks with garter ties.

Sporran: Plain leather day sporran.

Footwear: Brogues or some form of boot.

Jacket: Optional tweed.

Day Wear:

Shirt: Plain or patterned dress shirt, long sleeved with tie.

Hose: Plain color or shooting socks with garter ties.

Sporran: Leather day sporran or full mask fur.

Footwear: Brogues. Boots in some cases.

Jacket: Tweed or barathea wool or tartan to match.

Morning Dress:

Shirt: Plain or lightly patterned with solid or stripe tie.

Hose: Solid, darker in color with garter ties.

Sporran: Leather day sporran, full mask, some fur or hair sporrans possibly.

Footwear: Brogues.

Jacket: Darker tweed or black barathea. Waistcoat in tartan or tweed.

Black Tie:

Shirt: Marcella White cotton with turn down collar and black self-tie bow tie or jabot.

Hose: Diced or Argyll with flashes or ties.

Sporran: Full mask fur, fur, or hair.

Footwear: Black oxfords or buckle brogues.

Jacket: Black in an evening cut, matching or tartan waistcoat.

White Tie:

Shirt: Marcella White cotton with white tie or jabot.

Hose: Diced or Argyll with flashes or ties.

Sporran: Fur or hair.

Footwear: Buckle brogues.

Doublet: Black or tartan cut in an appropriate manner.

Appendix B: The Scottish Clans and their Chiefs

Below you will find a list of every major Clan and its Chief as of the date of this publication. To be considered a Clan a Chief of the Name and Arms of a family must be recognized by Lord Lyon King of Arms. Each Clan sends either their chief or a representative to the Standing Council of Scottish Chiefs. Those clans who no longer have a chief are considered Armigerous Families by the Court of Lord Lyon and the Standing Council and therefore not included in this list. A list of those families can be found in the following Appendix.

Agnew – Sir Crispin Agnew of Lochnaw Bt.

Anstruther – Toby Anstruther of that Ilk

Arthur – John MacArthur of that Ilk

Bannerman – Sir David Bannerman of Elsick Bt.

Barclay – Peter Barclay of that Ilk

Borthwick – Lord Borthwick

Boyle – The Earl of Glasgow

Brodie – Alexander Brodie of Brodie

Broun – Sir Wayne Broun of Colstoun Bt.

Bruce – The Earl of Elgin & Kincardine K.T.

Buchanan – John Michael Baillie-Hamilton of that Ilk and Arnprior

Burnett – James Burnett of Leys

Cameron – Donald Cameron of Lochiel

Campbell – His Grace The Duke of Argyll

Carmichael – Richard Carmichael of Carmichael

Charteris – The Earl of Wemyss And March

Chattan – John Mackintosh of Mackintosh

Chisholm – Hamish Chisholm of Chisholm

Cochrane – The Earl of Dundonald

Colquhoun – Sir Malcolm Colquhoun of Luss Bt.

Cranstoun – David Cranston of that Ilk

Currie – Robert Currie, Commander of the Name and Arms of Currie

Dalrymple – The Earl of Stair

Dewar – Michael Dewar of that Ilk

Drummond – Viscount Strathallan (Heir)

Dunbar – Sir James Dunbar of Mochrum Bt.

Dundas – David Dundas of Dundas

Crichton – David Crichton of that Ilk

Durie – Andrew Durie of Durie , CBE

Elliot – Madam Margaret Eliott of Redheugh

Elphinstone– Lord Elphinstone

Erskine – The Earl of Mar And Kellie

Ewen – Sir John McEwen Bt.

Ewing – Thor Ewing

Farquharson – Phillip Farquharson of Invercauld

Forsyth – Alistair Forsyth ygr of that Ilk

Fraser – The Lady Saltoun/ The Hon. Mrs Nicolson (Heir)

Fraser of Lovat – Lord Lovat

Gordon – The Marquess of Huntly

Graham – The Duke of Montrose

Grant – The Lord Strathspey

Gunn – Iain Gunn of Gunn

Guthrie – Alexander Guthrie of Guthrie

Haldane – Martin Haldane of Gleneagles

Hamilton – The Duke of Hamilton

Hannay – Professor David Hannay of Kirkdale and of that Ilk

Hay – The Earl of Erroll

Henderson – Alistair Henderson of Fordell

Hope – Sir Alexander Hope of Craighall Bt.

Hunter – Madam Pauline Hunter of Hunterson

Innes – The Duke of Roxburghe

Irvine – Alexander Irvine of Drum

Irving of Bonshaw – Rupert Irving of Bonshaw

Jardine – Sir William Jardine of Applegirth Bt.

Johnstone – The Earl of Annandale And Hartfell

Kennedy – The Marquess of Ailsa

Kerr – The Marquess of Lothian

Kincaid – Madam Arabella Kincaid of Kincaid

Lamont – Father Peter Noel Lamont (represented by Dr. George Burden)

Leask – Dr Jonathan Leask of that Ilk

Leslie – The Hon. Alexander Leslie (representative)

Lindsay – Earl of Lindsay

Lockhart – Ranald Lockhart of The Lee

Lumsden – Gillem Lumsden of that Ilk

Lyon – The Rt Hon. The Earl of Strathmore

MacDonald of Clanranald – The Captain of Clanranald

Macdonald of Glengarry – Patrick Macdonell of Glengarry(Presumed)

MacDonald of Keppoch – Ranald MacDonald of Keppoch

Macdonald of Macdonald – The Lord Macdonald of Macdonald

Macdonald of Sleat – Sir Ian Macdonald of Sleat Bt.

MacDougall – Morag MacDougall of MacDougall

Macdowall – Fergus Macdowall of Garthland

MacGillivray – Iain MacGillivray

MacGregor – Sir Malcolm MacGregor of MacGregor Bt.

MacIntyre – Duncan MacIntyre of Camus-na-h-Erie (Representative)

Maclachlan – Euan Maclachlan of Maclachlan

Mackay – The Hon. Elizabeth Fairbairn

Mackenzie – The Earl of Cromartie

Mackintosh – John Mackintosh of Mackintosh

MacLaine – Lorne Maclaine of Lochbuie

MacLaren – Donald MacLaren of MacLaren

Maclea – Niall Livingstone of Bachuil, Baron the Bachuil

MacLean – Major the Hon. Sir Lachlan MacLean of Duart and Morvern Bt.

MacLennan – Ruairidh MacLennan of MacLennan

Macleod of Raasay – John Macleod of Raasay

Macleod of the Lewes – Torquil Macleod of the Lewes

MacMillan – George MacMillan of MacMillan and Knap

Macnab – Jamie Macnab of Macnab

Macnaghten – Sir Malcolm Francis Macnaghten of MacNaghten Bt.

Macneacail – John Macneacail of Macneacail & Scorrabreac

Macneil – Roderick Macneil of Barra

Macpherson – James Macpherson of Cluny

MacTavish – Steven MacTavish of Dunardry

MacThomas – Andrew MacThomas of Finegand

Maitland – The Earl of Lauderdale

Malcolm (MacCallum) – Robin Malcolm of Poltalloch

Mar – The Countess of Mar

Marjoribanks – Andrew Marjoribanks of that Ilk

Matheson – Major Sir Alexander Matheson of Matheson, Bt.

McBain – Richard McBain of McBain

Moffat – Madam Jean Moffat of that Ilk

Moncreiffe – The Hon. Peregrine Moncreiffe of that Ilk

Montgomerie – The Earl of Eglinton & Winton

Morrison – Alasdair Morrison of Ruchdi

Munro – Hector Munro of Foulis

Napier – Lord Napier & Ettrick

Nesbitt – Mark Nesbitt of that Ilk

Ogilvy – The Earl of Airlie

Oliphant – Richard Oliphant of that Ilk

Pringle – Sir Norman Murray Pringle of that Ilk and Stichill

Ramsay – The Earl of Dalhousie

Riddell – Sir Walter John Buchanan Riddell Bt.

Robertson – Gilbert Robertson of Struan

Rollo – The Lord Rollo

Rose – David Rose of Kilravock

Ross – David Ross of Ross And Balnagowan

Scott – The Duke of Buccleuch KBE

Scott of Harden – Lord Polwarth

Scrymgeour – The Earl of Dundee

Sempill – The Lord Sempill

Shaw of Tordarroch – John Shaw of Tordarroch

Sinclair – The Earl of Caithness

Skene – Dugald Skene of Skene

Strange – Major Timothy Strange of Balcaskie

Sutherland – The Earl of Sutherland

Trotter – Major Alexander Trotter of Mortonhall, CVO

Urquhart – Colonel Wilkins Urquhart of Urquhart

Wallace – Andrew Wallace of that Ilk

Wedderburn – Lord Scrymgeour

Wemyss – Michael Wemyss of Wemyss

Appendix C: Scottish Armigerous Families

Those clans that have previously had a chief but who do not have a current chief are considered to be Armigerous Families. The recognised ones are listed below. Those names marked with an asterisk are at the time of publication in the process of selecting a new Chief. This is not an exhaustive list as it changes often.

Abercromby	Bell	Calder
Abernethy	Belshes	Caldwell
Adair	Bethune	Callender
Adam	Beveridge	Chalmers
Aikenhead	Binning	Cheyne
Ainslie	Bisset	Clelland
Aiton	Blackadder	Clephane
Anderson	Blackstock	Cockburn
Armstrong	Blair	Congilton
Arnott	Blane	Craig
Auchinleck	Blythe	Crawford
Ballie	Boswell	Crosbie
Baird	Brisbane	Dalmahoy
Balfour	Butter	Daziel
Bannatyne	Byres	Dennistoun
Baxter	Cairns	Don

Douglas	Gray	Learmonth
Duncan	Haliburton	Little
Dunlop	Halkerstone	Livingstone
Edmonstone	Halket	Logie
Fairlie	Hepburn	Lundin
Falconer	Heron	Lyle
Fenton	Herries	Macaulay
Fleming	Hog	MacBrayne
Fletcher	Hopkirk	MacDuff
Forrester	Horsburgh	MacFarlane
Fotheringham	Houston	MacFie
Fullarton	Hutton	MacGillivray*
Galbraith	Inglis	MacInne
Galloway	Kelly	Mackie
Garden	Kinloch	MacClellan
Gartshore	Kinnaird	MacQuarrie
Gayre	Kinnear	MacQueen
Ged	Kinnimont	Macrae
Gibsone	Kirkcaldy	Masterton
Gladstains	Kirkpatrick	Maule
Glas	Laing	Maxton
Glen	Lammie	Maxwell
Glendinning	Langlands	McCorquodale

McCulloch	Pennycook	Strachan
McIver	Pentland	Straiton
McKerrell	Pitblado	Sydserf
Meldrum	Pitcairn	Symmers
Melville	Pollock	Tailyour
Mercer	Polwarth	Tait
Middleton	Porterfield	Tennant
Moncur	Preston	Troup
Monteith	Purves	Turnbull
Monypenny	Rait	Tweedie
Mouat	Ralston	Udny
Moubray	Renton	Vans
Mow	Roberton	Walkinshaw
Muir	Rossie	Wardlaw
Nairn	Russel	Watson
Nevoy	Rutherford	Wauchope
Newlands	Schaw	Weir
Newton	Seton	Whitefoord
Norvel	Skirving	Whitelaw
Ochterlony	Somerville	Wishart
Orrock	Spalding	Wood
Paisley	Spottiswood	Young
Paterson	Stewart	

Appendix D: Plant Badges

Below you will find a list of the common plant badges used by various clans and families. Plant badges may be worn by any clansman behind the badge in the bonnet. In most instances a simple sprig of the flower or leaf is sufficient. This list names the scientific name of each plant where it is pertinent, as many common names of flora are shared in the English language but some species differ between the British Isles and North America. One example of this is the (Red) Whortleberry, which in North America is called a Cranberry, and in Europe the Lingonberry. Some common names are used for the same plant, as is the case in Scots Pine and Scots Fir; both of which refer to *Pinus sylvestris*. Some common names are used for these plant badges are unique to a clan but have no exact taxonomical match for it, these are marked with an Asterix* and have the common name of the genius displayed beside them instead. Some are so common however that multiply varieties of species exist and thus would be either insufficient or redundant to limit these, as has been done for the several coloured roses used by several clans.

Alpin – Scots Pine: *Pinus sylvestris*

Anstruther – Olive: *Olea europaea*

Barclay – Mayflower: *Epigaea repens*

Borthwick – Red Rose

Boyd – (Common) Laurel: *Prunus laurocerasus*

Bruce – Rosemary: *Salvia rosmarinus*

Buchan – Sunflower: *Helianthus annuus*

Buchanan – Birch*

Burnett – Holly: *Ilex aquifolium*

Cameron – Oak: *Quercus robur*

Campbell – Bog Myrtle: *Myrica gale*

Chisolm – Fern*

Chattan – Red Whortleberry (Cranberry): *Vaccinium vitis-idaea*

Colquhoun – Hazel*

Cumming – Cumin: *Cuminum cyminum*

Cranstoun – Strawberry*

Drummond – Holly: *Ilex aquifolium*

Elliot – White Hawthorn: *Crataegus monogyna*

Farquharson – Seedling Scots Fir: *Pinus sylvestris*

Fergusson – Poplar (Aspen) Seedlings

Forbes – Broom: *Cytisus scoparius*

Forrester – Oak: *Quercus robur*

Forsyth – Forsythia

Fraser – Yew: *Taxus baccata*

Gordon – Rock Ivy: *Hedera helix*

Graham – Spurge Laurel: *Daphne laureola*

Grant – Scots Pine: *Pinus sylvestris*

Gunn – Juniper: *Juniperus communis*

Grierson – Bluebell: *Hyacinthoides non-scripta*

Hannay – Periwinkle: *Catharanthus roseus*

Hay – Mistletoe: *Viscum album*

Henderson – Cotton Grass: *Eriophorum*

Home – Broom: *Genisteae*

Hunter – Thrift: *Armeria Maritima*

Innes – Great Bulrush: *Schoenoplectus tabernaemontani*

Jardine – Apple Blossom*

Johnston – Red Hawthorne: *Crataegus monogyna*

Kieth – White Rose

Kennedy – Oak: *Quercus robur*

Lamont – Crab Apple*

Lennox – Red Rose

Leslie – Rue: *Ruta graveolens*

Lindsay – Lime*

Lumsden – Hazel*

MacBain – Boxwood: *Buxus sempervirens*

Macdonald of Macdonald – Common Heather: *Calluna vulgaris*

MacDougal – Bell Heather: *Erica cinerea*

MacDowall – Oak: *Quercus robur*

MacGregor – Scots Pine: *Pinus sylvestris*

Macinnes – Holly: *Ilex aquifolium*

MacIntyre – White Heather: *Calluna vulgaris**

MacKay – Great Bullrush: *Schoenoplectus tabernaemontani*

MacKenzie – Stagshorn Clubmoss: *Lycopodium clavatum clavatum*

MacKinnon – St. John's Wort*

MacKintosh – Red Whortleberry (Cranberry): *Vaccinium vitis-idaea*

MacLachlan – Rowan*

MacLennan – Furze: *Ulex gallii*

MacLeod – Juniper*

MacMillan – Holly: *Ilex aquifolium*

MacNab – Stone Bramble: *Rubus saxatilis*

MacNaughten – Trailing Azalea: *Kalmia procumbens*

MacNeil – Dryas: *Dryas octopetala*

MacPherson – White Heather: *Calluna vulgaris**

MacThomas – Snowberry: *Symphoricarpos*

Maitland – Honeysuckle: *Lonicera periclymenum*

Matheson – Yellow Rose*

Menzies – Menzies Heath*

Moncrieff – Oak: *Quercus robur*

Morrison – Driftweed*

Munro – Common Club Moss: *Lycopodium clavatum*

Murray – Juniper and Butcher's Broom*

Nicolson – Juniper*

Ogilvy – Hawthorn: *Crataegus monogyna*

Oliphant – Bulrush or Sycamore*

Donnachaidh – Bracken: *Pteridium**

Rose – Wild Rosemary: *Andromeda polifolia*

Ross – Juniper*

Scott – Blaeberry: *Vaccinium myrtillus*

Scrymgeour – Rowan*

Sinclair – Whin: *Ulex minor**

Stewart – Oak: *Quercus robur*

Sutherland – Cotton-sedge: *Eriophorum*

Urquhart – Wallflower: *Erysimum*

Wallace – Oak: *Quercus robur*

Wedderburn – Beech*

Appendix E: A Guide to Ladies Tartan Sashes

The most recognizable form of ladies Highland dress as seen today, not only because of its wide usage with country dancers but also because of its all around versatility, is the tartan sash. The sash is usually about 10" to 12" in width and about three or so yards in length and can be woven in a lightweight tartan material or in silk. It can be worn in four distinct ways, as found on the following pages with descriptions.

Married Clanswomen: The first way to wear a sash is wrapped around under the left arm and pinned at the *right* shoulder, this form is appropriate for clanswomen wearing their husband's tartan. It can be affixed with any sort of women's brooch. You may also wear it back where both pieces of tartan are worn on the back instead of one hanging down in the front and one in the back, this is often done after dinner for dancing.

Unmarried Clanswomen: This style is for those unmarried clanswomen who wish to show their tartan, it may also be worn by a married clanswoman who wishes to display her clans tartan. This is the simplest of styles where the sash is worn over the *right* shoulder and then secured at the left hip. Normally the sash is tied into a bow or rosette to secure it and a brooch is placed on the knot. Some tartan sashes are too thick to be tied into a knot like this so it may be necessary to make a false bow. This can be done by pinning the sash together then adding a second pin about four to six inches below the first, then bringing the two parts together with the brooch giving the illusion of a tied bow.

For Dancing: This style is most common with Scottish country dancers and is probably the best for dancing as it does not interfere with any of the movements of the dance. This style is also useful for those ladies who are entitled to wear the sashes or stars of orders of chivalry as it does not interfere with the front of the dress. The sash is folded in half and is then either pleated together and pinned with a brooch or is brought into a rosette and pinned with a brooch. You can either let the tails hang or pin them to the back of the dress.

Wives of Chiefs, Chieftains, and Colonels: This last style is reserved for the wives of Chiefs, Chieftains, and the wives of Colonels of Highland regiments; as well as women who are chiefs in their own right. You will also see certain ladies of the court and members of the Royal Family wear their sashes in this style at balls. It is worn over the left shoulder in the same manner as a clanswoman but in reverse.

Appendix F: The Wearing of Decorations and Awards with Highland Dress

For those men and women who have served in the armed forces of their country, or those who are members of an order of chivalry, or those who are members of clubs or societies where awards are given in the form of a medal there are several conventions to wearing these medals with Traditional Highland Dress. When debating when to wear medals the quickest thing you can do is to check the invitation. Most semi-formal and formal function invitations will specify medals or no medals. In the case that it is not specified ask yourself if it is a military or some form of veterans function. If so, it's likely appropriate to wear them. In all cases only miniature chest medals are worn with Black and White tie, full sized chest medals can be worn with day wear, and at veterans or remembrance functions, but never wear full sized medals with your formal Highland wear (with the exception of neck medals/collars and breast stars, which can be worn with black and white tie, in combination with miniature chest medals). Miniatures are typically worn on the lapel of a jacket or doublet for men, and on the breast of a dress for women. Breast stars should be placed wherever the order it is from specified. Neck devices should be worn close up under the bowtie or over the jabot, they should not hang freely like a sports medal. It is advised that you do not mix the medals of clubs, societies or fraternities with military awards (and in many countries it is against regulation). Orders of chivalry as used in the British and Commonwealth systems of honor can be worn in conjunction with military awards as the systems are integrated. If you are from the United States or another country and wish to mix medals consult your nation's uniform regulations. For additional guidance, pick up a copy of *Spink's Guide to the Wearing of Orders, Decorations and Medals*.

Appendix G: Highland Wear "Under Arms"

In some clan and society functions, civilians, or more properly, persons in civilian clothing, may be asked to undertake certain ceremonial duties such as carrying a banner or leading a small parade. Often there is a pseudo military component to these things, and as always there are long standing conventions and traditions which I hope to outline below.

In a procession where a banner is to be carried there are a fair number of conventions that one should be aware of. Firstly, though we should cover some elements of dressing for this sort of occasion. In a day wear setting, such as a games or clan gathering, wear the appropriate dress code of the day. If you are carrying a flag, sword, or some other ceremonial object, it is appropriate to wear your bonnet, even if indoors, while completing this task. Banners of organizations or nations should be carried ahead of your "formation", these can be of course flanked by "guards", but they should always be forward of the host. Banners of arms of individuals should always be carried behind the bearers of these arms. Furthermore, if a chief's representative is present for your clan or society, their pinsel should be carried ahead of any other present armigers banner, with them falling in behind in order of seniority. Any sort of ceremonial item should be carried ahead of flags with whoever the senior dignitary may be.

When passing a review stand a standard military salute should not be rendered, a 'present arms' with a sword or some other form of acknowledgment to whomever is taking the salute by the leading flags guards is encouraged however. It is also encouraged for those bearing clan or society flags and banners of arms to "dip" their flags in a respectful manner; as the review stand may have a chief or some other games dignitary present (it is also often the location of the National Flag or Royal Banner as well).

Glossary of Terms Associated with Highland Dress

Apron: The front part of the kilt, lies flat and is secured at the left-hand side.

Argyll: A style of jacket, cut like a blazer but short for highland wear. May be of the Braemar style with scalloped pockets and gauntlet cuffs, or Crail style- plain cuffs and pockets.

Armiger: Any individual who bears their own personal coat of arms.

Balmoral: A round brimmed knitted bonnet, felted and worn with a cockade and badge.

Basting Stitch: A light stitch put into the pleats when making a kilt to be removed when finished.

Barbour Jacket: An outdoor jacket, often made of treated canvas for foul weather conditions, can be worn with a kilt.

Bias: In fabric terms, the diagonal of a piece of fabric, to be "on the bias" is to have the fabric turned 45 degrees.

Bias Cut: Fabric set to the diagonal, see Bias.

Black Tie: Traditionally the least formal mode of dress in the formal wear spectrum, now seen as the default and categorized by the wearing of a black bowtie.

Bonnet: Any form of Highland or Lowland head dress.

Braemar: Often the term ascribed to a style of Argyll jacket wherein the pocket flaps are scalloped and the cuffs are in the gauntlet style.

Cairngorm Stone: A semi-precious stone, yellow-green in color and often used to decorate broches, pins, pommels, etc.

Cantle: The top part of a sporran, can be functioning or nonfunctioning, and is usually of metal or wood.

Clan: Any major Scottish family that has a recognised chief.

Coatee: A formal jacket cut short at the true waist. For example, Prince Charlie.

Court Dress: The most formal mode of dress in the formal spectrum. Used only for special state functions.

Court of the Lord Lyon: The Heraldic Authority of Scotland, as such regulates all matters on heraldry and is the formal recogniser of the Clan Chiefs. Comprised of the Lord Lyon King of Arms, the Sovereigns highest representative in Scotland, and his or her Officers of Arms.

Crail: A style of day wear jacket most similar to the saxon cut blazer.

Cromach: Also called a crook or cromag, the traditional Scottish walking stick. Should reach the armpit of the user and have a curved head of wood or horn.

Day Wear: The everyday mode of dress in highland wear. Consists of a tweed jacket, kilt, coloured hose, leather sporran, and sturdy shoes.

Dirk: The traditional Scottish dagger, now worn for special occasions as an accessory or decoration.

Doublet: A formal jacket that has tashes or is double breasted. Examples are the Regulation Doublet and Montrose.

Edwardian Era: The period between 1901-10, the Reign of Edward VII.

Flashes: Strips of cloth secured by a garter as decoration, worn with hose.

Full Formal: See White Tie.

Garter Ties: Strips of woven wool used to tie and secure hose.

Gauntlet Cuff: Any cuff where the cuff of the jacket appears to be turned back to create a cuff around the circumference of a sleeve.

Ghillie: A Scottish outdoor guide/estate worker.

Glengarry: A kind of highland bonnet more common in the Victorian and Edwardian periods. Shaped like a garrison cap and worn at an angle, and often worn by pipers and military personnel, though acceptable for civilian use.

Harris Tweed Authority: The body responsible for regulating the tweed industry in Scotland.

Highland Revival: The period around the turn of the 18th century and into the mid 19th century, wherein public interest in Scottish culture boomed in popularity and many old traditions were revived or refined. Aided immensely by persons like Sir Walter Scott, Robert Burns, and the Royal Family.

Hose: The traditional kilt sock, made in a variety of colors and patterns.

Jabot: An ornamental frill collar, often made of lace and worn in place of a black or white tie. Acceptable in both modes of dress.

Kilmarnock: A variation of the Balmoral bonnet.

Kilt: The pleated skirt of the Scottish National Dress worn by men.

Kilt Belt: A wide belt for day or formal usage with Highland wear as a decoration. Kilt Belts should not secure the Kilt to the body.

Kilt Pin: A decorative pin worn on the right side of the apron between one-third and half way up the apron.

Kilt Socks: See hose.

Market Stick: A shorter form of the Cromach, found all over the British Isles.

Morning Dress: Formal Day Wear.

Mourning Dress: Day Wear as used in a time of Mourning or Remembrance. Often characterized by a Black neck tie, jacket, or mourning cuff.

Norfolk Jacket: The Tweed saxon wear shooting jacket. Often Belted with gussets on the back.

Plaid: A large piece of heavyweight tartan around 2-4 meters in length used often as a blanket or matchcoat. Can also refer to variations on this for formal wear such as a piper's plaid or belted plaid.

Rise: The posterior measurement in tailoring to determine where a garment sits in relation to one's natural waist.

Saxon Wear: Standard English/Western fashion, anything non-highland wear.

Scottish Tartans Authority: The body responsible for regulating the Scottish tartan industry, operates the Scottish Register of Tartans.

Selvedge: The woven edge of a piece of fabric.

Semi Formal: See Black Tie.

Sett: The sequenced thread count of tartan.

Sgian Achlais: Similar to a Sgian Dubh though longer, traditionally worn on the inside of the jacket and often used more like a hunting knife.

Sgian Dubh: The small fixed blade knife worn in the kilt hose on the wearer's dominant side. Can be functional or purely decorative.

Sporran: The Scottish purse or bag worn by men. Usually suspended by a strap or chain secured around the waist and hung on the apron side of the kilt. Can be functional or decorative.

Tartan: Woolen fabric woven in a pattern of two or more colors.

Tashes: Shall decorative flaps that hang off the backs and sides of some formal Highland jackets.

Tattersall: A pattern of fabric used for daywear shirts, often on a white or light coloured base with thin lines in one or more colors intersecting.

Thumb Stick: A walking stick somewhere between waist and chest height with a forked head, similar to a shooting stick.

Tourie: The small yarn ball on top of a Scottish bonnet.

Trews: High waisted tartan trousers, also a Scots term for any trousers.

Tweed: A rough woolen fabric woven in the U.K. often plain, patterned, or flecked with color.

Victorian Era: Roughly the second half of the 19th century during the reign of Queen Victoria.

Waist Belt: A narrow belt meant to be worn with trousers. Can also be used under a waistcoat to suspend a Dirk.

Waistcoat: A vest, made without sleeves to be worn under a jacket. Can be cut kilt length in a normal pointed hem, hemmed straight across, or can be made with a trapezoid shaped cutaway for the sporran.

White Tie: Full formal wear. Marked by the white bowtie, stiff fronted shirt, and/or the lace jabot.

Sources

Published works:

Erskine, The Hon. Stuart Ruaidri, *The Kilt and How to Wear it*, 1901

Innes of Learney, Sir Thomas, and Johnston and Bacon, *The Scottish Tartans: Histories of the Clans, Chiefs arms, and Clansmen's badges*, Stirling 1963(1999 Reprint)

MacDonald, Peter Eslea, *The 1819 Key Pattern Book – One Hundred Original Tartans*, Crieff 2012

MacKinnon of Dunakin, C.R.,FSA Scot, *Tartans and Highland Dress*, Glasgow 1961

Maclean, Charles, *The Clan Almanac: A Complete Guide to Scottish Family Names*, New York 1990

McGuire, Dr. Colin P. and MacDonald, Nathan B. FSA Scot, *Traditional Highland Civilian Dress: A Definition and Guide with Visual Examples*, 2020, Originally published on Xmarksthescot.com 2014

McIntyre North, Charles Niven, *The Book of the Club of True Highlanders*, 1881

Way of Plean, George and Squire Romilly, *Scottish Clan and Family Encyclopedia*, New York 1998

Internet Resources:

Albanach.org, accessed 2022

Angelfire.com, Tom Mungall Highland Wear, accessed 2022

Clanchiefs.org.uk, accessed 2022

Tartansauthority.com, August 2022

Traditional Kilters, Facebook group, created 2016

Xmarksthescot.com threads, accessed 2022

Other:

Disarming Act, 1746

www.ingramcontent.com/pod-product-compliance
Lightning Source LLC
Chambersburg PA
CBHW051616010526
44107CB00037B/1444/J